He Died Twice

Sholeh Shabangiz

Order this book online at www.trafford.com
or email orders@trafford.com

Most Trafford titles are also available at major online book retailers.

Note for Librarians: A cataloguing record for this book is available from Library and Archives Canada at www.collectionscanada.ca/amicus/index-e.html

Printed in Victoria, BC, Canada.

ISBN: 9781-4120-9909-7 (sc)
ISBN: 978-1-4269-1635-9 (hc)

Our mission is to efficiently provide the world's finest, most comprehensive book publishing service, enabling every author to experience success.
To find out how to publish your book, your way, and have it available worldwide, visit us online at www.trafford.com

Trafford rev. 09/16/09

 www.trafford.com

North America & international
toll-free: 1 888 232 4444 (USA & Canada)
phone: 250 383 6864 ♦ fax: 812 355 4082

I dedicate this book;

To my parents: for your unlimited support and unconditional love. I love you both with all my heart.

To my two sisters: Time away from you is time lost. I wish you were near.

To my three children: in my heart for you, I carry extreme love and yet, so much guilt.

To Kayvan: There isn't a day that I don't think of you.

To Kamran: Many thanks for all your support.

To Katayoon: Thanks for being my daughter.

To my grandparents: for making childhood memories all fun.

To Ali: a candle in the wind, gone too soon. We miss you.

Chapter 1

*M*y grandmother Fariba seemed like an ordinary woman who lived a very simple life. The truth of the matter is her life was anything but simple. Beneath her seemingly calm appearance, she had lived a tormented life. A tale obscured silently and perfectly deep inside her, in the burial chamber of her heart.

Grandma was a role model to me in so many ways. I wanted to be like her. I always felt more connected to her than to my own mom, her daughter Sepideh. My mother gave me all the things I needed, but grandma was everything I wanted. I cherished everything about her; the way she laughed, the elegance in the way she dressed or did her hair, the way she walked, the soft melody in her voice, I treasured it all and I wanted to know more. The desire to know her better had pushed me to wait patiently for the day to come when she would open the pages of her life's book, to share its contents, to let me write her story. It was a journey to her past. A voyage to the most concealed part of her life—the part she kept hidden from most people. I pursued her so many times on that matter, and every time she answered, "No." I remember one conversation I had with her on that subject vividly.

"My dear Azale, why do you ask me to talk about my past?"

"I believe your story needs to be heard, grandma."

"Why? There is nothing about it that needs to be told. It's just another life, lived and forgotten."

"Is it really forgotten?"

"It better be. Nothing good can come out by telling useless stories."

"That's where you're wrong grandma. Time has changed so many things in this country, but still there are things that may happen the same way. I believe by telling your story you can help lots of women."

"How much do you know about my life anyway?"

"I have heard pieces of it from mom, but not all. It's a puzzle and I want to put all the pieces together."

"But why now?"

"I have been asking you for a long time grandma."

I recall grandma being quiet so I continued, "Think about it again, grandma. You don't have to answer me now; think it through. I believe your story deserves to be heard."

I left her without having much hope for any answer other than a "no" as she had always given me. I couldn't believe my ears when, two days later, she called ready to tell it, and to tell it all.

⌒

The night before my meeting with grandma I couldn't sleep. Next morning, I arrived early; the magical day with grandma had finally come. The early morning sun made everything glitter. The road shimmered and her house looked more beautiful than ever. Animated, energetic and eager to start, I rang the bell. She opened the door and welcomed me with a warm embrace. I followed her into the living room. She lit her scented candles as she always did and sat on her old antique chair across from the sofa where I chose to sit. The white curtain behind her danced in silence as it floated in the air with each breeze. Her white chadoor* hung from her shoulders down to her toes. A white shawl covered her head and a few strands of gray hair had escaped to frame her lovely, beautiful face. Although time had left its footprints on her features, her beauty, could not easily be hidden, nor forgotten behind the mask of age. She seemed comfortable and calm. Her moment of truth had arrived:

"It was September; I finished high school three months earlier in June. Back then at eighteen, I was pretty; full of life and energy, a daydreamer, a girl with unlimited imagination and yet, a very limited life." Grandma paused, reliving those memories for a few seconds.

"I remember the day so clearly, a day with sapphire sky, pleasant breeze and the smell of lilacs that filled the air. It was a beautiful summer evening when I first saw him. I can still see it as if it happened yesterday. That day, I met the man whose existence changed my life forever and gave a new meaning to the world I knew.

Minoo, one of my high school friends, had invited our other friend Leila and me for an afternoon tea party. That was a routine between us friends; we used to gather at each other's houses once a month for tea and pastries. When the party ended, I decided to walk back home instead of calling for a cab, I lived close by and I loved to walk. On the way back, a few blocks away from my house, I stopped for a moment to look at a pair of beautiful shoes in a store's window. Those blue shiny shoes had haunted me for the past month. Just as any other day, I pulled my chadoor up, up to my ankles, so that I could imagine and visualize those shoes on my feet. Only this time, when I finally turned my head away from the window, I saw him. He stood a few steps away, looking at me the same way I looked at those shoes, as if I were the prettiest thing he'd ever seen. For a moment, our eyes

---

* Chadoor – a long veil that cover the head all the way down to the toe. In Islamic countries it is customary for women to wear chadoor to cover their body.

met. His sharp stare pierced through me like needles and I felt a rush of heat through my body.

Almost immediately, I tried to cover my feet. I felt nervous and my hands were shaking. The chadoor slipped from my head, exposing my long black hair. Quickly, he stepped forward and helped adjust the chadoor. I felt so embarrassed that I started to walk away without even thanking him. As I walked, he didn't say anything, but I could still feel the heavy weight of his eyes on me. 'Why did he look at me like that?' I wondered.

But somehow deep down in my heart, I liked it, just like any other girl of my age would have. I didn't turn around to look at him, even though I wanted very badly to do so. When I reached home, I could still feel my cheeks burning, as if they were on fire.

"Look at me; even now the thought of it makes me blush." Grandma giggled like a child. Then, she continued:

Still nervous, I went inside the house and shut the door.

"Fariba is that you?" I heard Mama. I entered the living room and saw Mama sitting on her floral sofa, knitting, one of her favorite activities.

"Yes, Mama, it's me."

'Why is my voice shaking?' I wondered.

"How was the party?" Mama asked.

"Wasn't bad…. Is Papa home yet?"

"Yes, darling, he's in the basement, fixing the grass cutting machine."

I was so glad that Mama didn't notice the wobble in my voice.

"Fariba, can I have your lavender shirt now?" Ferry, my sister asked as she rushed, a little too quickly, into our living room. Although only two years younger than me, Ferry always acted more childish.

"No, you can't have my shirt," I answered. "How many times are you going to bother me for it?"

"I'll bother you as long as it takes." Ferry was determined.

"Well, you're wasting your time and energy."

"But this morning you told me that I could have it after you returned from the party."

"I changed my mind. Now leave me alone."

"But you said…Mama…she promised me…"

"Okay, girls, that is enough," Mama interrupted. *"Ferry, I wish you would stop that for now. You behave like a little child sometimes."*

"Stupid, if you ask me," I chided.

"Fariba, stop it. You're not being so nice yourself and I don't want to hear more about this." Mama's tone forced Ferry and I to stay quiet.

"Good, now I'm going to set the dinner table. Who wants to help?" Mama got up from the sofa and walked toward the kitchen. Ferry and I followed her without saying a word.

In the kitchen, at the table, my ten-year-old sister Zina looked annoyed next to my very spoiled, five year old brother Zafa whom I used to call 'The Demolisher'. He kept asking Zina to color a picture of a cat.

"Kids, get up and take your painting papers and pencils to your room. We want to set the table," I ordered.

To my surprise, they followed my instructions with no resistance. Very often, they needed a few of my shouts before they listened to anything I had to say. At that age, I didn't want to deal with my younger siblings. I didn't have patience for them and I couldn't figure out how Mama had that much understanding. She was very tolerant of Zina and Zafa. Mama had always been a very kind woman. She devoted her life to her little family and I never heard her complain about anything. Her belief in God and the power of prayer had always surprised me. *"Everything happens for a reason. God knows best,"* she used to say. She had her own unique ways of doing things. Her medium size bone structure and her big almond shaped eyes were a heritage from her Persian mother. But her strong jaw line and pointed nose were bequest from her father and his Russian ancestors.

Mama loved to embellish the rooms; therefore, our house always looked neat and nicely decorated. She spent most of her time in the kitchen: cooking, baking and cleaning. I remember when my parents *started to build the house; she insisted on a very large kitchen with lots of wooden, spacious cabinets.*

Ferry had a lot of Mama's genes in her. She looked so much like Mama, except that Ferry was the tomboy of the family. She wore jeans most of the time and preferred to keep her hair short.

I, on the other hand, looked more like papa. I had his nose and his big brown eyes, even the shape of my lips were more similar to Papa's. Physically and emotionally speaking, I had more things in common with him; except for my medium size bone structure which I took from Mama. Papa looked more slender because of his tallness, long legs, and narrow shoulders. He had inherited that from his father along with grandpa's salt and pepper's hair. As long as I remembered, Papa's hair looked that way.

Papa taught literature in high school and did tutoring every day after work. He was the only bread winner of our family. An old-fashioned kind of guy, he never believed in the notion of a wife working outside of the home. But he never degraded what women did at home.

"A woman has a big job, don't ever kid yourself," he always argued with other men who believed they were the only ones with a job in their household. "Her job is at home; we work outside and women work inside, and it's all the same," he used to say.

He made all the rules. Of course, we had to obey and we always did. He was very firm and, at the same time, very gentle in his own way. My Papa, I remember him being well respected and well loved.

Papa always told us: "Don't ever let me show you my mean side, behave properly." Somehow we never saw his mean side…well, except for one time and I will get to that later.

I remember that night very well. At the table, I was more quiet than usual, but not in a way to raise any questions. Although, physically, I sat there at that table in our house with my family, my mind couldn't have been any farther away. Wondering about that boy and traveling to where his eyes met mine, to where he looked at me in a way I wanted to be looked at. I didn't feel nervous any more.

In fact, somehow I was happy about my little encounter with him. Something about that face, about his eyes and the way he looked at me, it lit my heart up like a burning candle and kept me wide awake most of that night. As I thought about him more and more, I realized that all I could picture in my mind was his face and nothing else. I passed him by so fast, scared and nervous, that I didn't even look at him completely. I couldn't remember anything about him, only his undeniable face and mesmerizing eyes.

The next morning, I decided to get out of the house, hoping that I would see him again. I needed to come up with a good excuse. I thought of something fast: "Mama, may I go to the mall?"

"Why this early? The stores won't open until ten."

"I won't call for a taxi, I'll walk. That way, by the time I reach the mall, it will be ten o'clock."

"What do you need from there anyway?"

"I want to buy a poster for my room."

"Fariba, we can hardly see the walls of your room. They are all covered by posters already." True, but did I want to admit that? I didn't think so.

"Please, Mama, I saw a beautiful poster yesterday. It's a picture of an ocean in the sunset."

"I don't know where you're going to put that poster, but you can go. Remember to come back before your father gets home for lunch."

Oh, it was easier than I thought; she wanted me to be home before Papa and he wasn't going to be home before noon. She had basically given me permission to stay out for a couple of hours. I felt excited. 'Surely I would see the boy again.' I thought. Impatient, I almost ran out of the house with my slippers instead of my shoes.

Two hours later, I returned home with no luck. 'Why was I so sure that he would be there, waiting for me? Why was I certain that he wanted to see me again? Why did I have to see him anyway?' I asked myself all those questions. Only, I couldn't come up with a good answer. All I knew was that somehow I needed to see his face again. 'Maybe he works during the day.' I found an explanation for myself.

Yes, he was probably at work, and I would go out in the evening next time. My plan was formed.

Later that day, I found another reason to leave the house. Surprisingly, Mama didn't ask too many questions. I went out that evening and looked at every face, but none was the one I wanted. I wasn't able to find those piercing hazel eyes. After that day, I went out every chance I could get, and every time, I hoped to see him once more. A month passed and, after finding no trace of him, I knew I had to give up that girlish dream—and I almost did.

Then, one day in early November, when I had just stepped out the house to take a bus to Zina's school, I saw him again. He was standing at the corner of Mir Avenue and Apadana Street, one block away from our house. My knees started to tremble like they never had before. I felt happy and yet so tense at the same time.

I wanted to look at him, to let my heart take note of every inch of him. But for some reason, I couldn't look; it felt very awkward. I couldn't clearly understand why I couldn't look at him when every cell in my body yearned and searched for him. I think it must have been the way girls were brought up in a Muslim country. A girl was not to look at a man in such a way; it was a forbidden act, a shameful behavior. Weren't we told: 'Girls shouldn't look at men, at least, not eye to eye?' As a result, I started to walk up the block without looking at him.

'Look at him, Fariba,' my heart yelled at me.

'Why can't I look at him now?' I questioned myself.

'Fariba, look; take your eyes off the asphalt and look at him,' my heart ordered.

'But you shouldn't,' my brain advised me. Angry at myself, I listened to the bloody debate between my heart and my brain. I had waited for this moment the whole month and I had promised myself to stare him in the eye and even smile if I ever saw him again. Instead, I felt so shy and nervous, as a five-year-old child would be.

As I got steadily closer, my hands started to shake and became sweaty while my fingertips turned cold as ice. 'What if my veil fall off again? Oh wouldn't that be a real disaster? I'd rather die instead.'

I kept thinking. I prayed to God that he wouldn't see through me, that he would not be able to read my mind. 'Is he looking at me?' I wondered and hoped not.

When I reached him, my heart couldn't fit inside my chest. I passed him in a trance, as in slow motion and only then I heard his voice for the first time.

"I need to talk to you," he suddenly whispered.

He wanted to talk to me. 'What should I do now, Should I answer him or not?' I asked myself. 'You shouldn't answer him Fariba.' But why not?

The war between my brain and my heart continued and of course, my brain won, it always did, well, not always but for most part it did. My winner brain had told me not to answer, so I didn't answer and continued to walk. 'Oh, God what could he possibly want to tell me?' I thought about that question and came up with at least ten different answers.

'Stop and turn back to him,' my deepest desire yelled. 'He wants to talk, stop,' the inner voice yelled again. But my legs had a mind of their own; they kept walking.

He started to walk, a few steps away behind me, all the way to the bus station, and there, he stood close as I waited for the bus. I wanted him to say something again, but he didn't. Finally the bus arrived; my heart ached and I wanted to cry. I didn't want to leave; I wanted to scream at him and say, "Why didn't you say another word?" But, despite the storm inside me, I remained quiet.

As I put my foot on the first step to get inside the bus, he held my arm gently and whispered against my left ear.

"Please call me," he said as he handed me a piece of paper. I thought I wouldn't take the paper from him. But I guess my hands were not following my thoughts because my hand took the paper as I went inside the bus. The bus started to move, but I couldn't. Why couldn't I move? Why didn't my body parts work with me as a team? I wondered.

As the bus pulled me away, I stood right behind the door and watched him intensely. At the same time, I held onto that piece of paper, as if my life depended on it. I could visualize him in my head and this time, my heart took the whole picture. He was tall. His wide shoulders made him look like an athlete. He had olive skin and dark brown hair, perfectly styled; parting on top from the left, leaving a few strands on the forehead with the two sides nicely combed toward the back. His dark, thick eyebrows drew the attention right to his hazel eyes. The most handsome man I had ever seen. He was young, maybe in the mid-twenties. His casual dark blue jacket and his light blue jeans looked good on him.

Soon, I realized that I hadn't even looked at that piece of paper he gave me. I opened it with my sweaty hands. There was a telephone number with a name underneath; his name was Pooya.

My life was never the same from that moment on. I didn't know what to do. 'Should I call him, or should I not?' I debated as usual. I used to do that a lot those days, fighting with myself in my head. I asked myself so many questions:

'What if he thinks of me as an easy, ill repute girl?' Girls in Iran were not supposed to do that. 'What if I call him and my parents find out that I talked to a boy?' What if this…? What if that….

Pure madness, I couldn't make up my mind. Well, of course I wanted to call him, but it felt uncomfortable to do so. But then I thought, being uncomfortable is nothing compared to the pleasure it would bring me. That did it; I made up my mind. I would just call him. I would talk to him and then we would say goodbye and never talk again. 'Anything wrong with that?' I questioned. 'No, I don't think so.' And so, I convinced myself.

Next, I needed to wait for a time when I could have the house all to myself. Up until then, I never realized how crowded our house always was—never empty, always somebody there. That never bothered me before, but now it did. Finally, after waiting through three long days, God answered my prayer.

"Fariba?"

"Yes Mama?"

"I have to take your grandpa to his doctor's appointment for a checkup. The kids are coming with me, but I want you to stay here so you can warm up your dad's food when he gets home."

"Okay, Mama."

Perfect. That was exactly what I had waited for.

"Maybe I should leave Zina with you," Mama said.

Oh no, Zina was a tattle-tale. I had to make Mama take her along, too.

"No Mama. I want to have some peace around here. Zina will bother me a lot."

"When did I bother you? You're a liar!" Zina ran in to object.

"I'm not."

"You are too."

"You always bother me. In fact—"

"Okay, Okay. I'll take Zina with me," Mama interrupted me. "Why do you have such an attitude toward your sister?"

I didn't answer her. I just wanted them to leave the house before Papa came back. As soon as they left, I picked up the phone and dialed Pooya's number.

It was the beginning of something so wonderful. I remember our first phone conversation almost word for word, and the way his gentle voice stirred me the moment he answered.

"Hello?" the voice said on the other end of the line.

"Hello...hi. Is this Pooya?" I asked timidly.

"Yes, this is he."

Suddenly, I became so nervous. I didn't know what to say anymore. I wanted to hang up and I would have done that, but he didn't give me a chance; He started to talk.

"I wondered if you would call. I'm glad that you did, Fariba."

Fariba? How did he know my name? As far as I remembered, I had never told him that.

"How do you know my name?" I asked curiously.

"The other day, do you believe we saw each other for the first time?"

"Do you mean by the shoe store? Yes we did, didn't we?"

"Yes and no."

"I'm sorry; I don't understand."

"I saw you way before that, but you acknowledged me then for the first time."

"Still, you didn't answer my question," I said.

"You asked about how I knew your name, Right?"

"Right, I never told you what my name was."

"I saw you in the beginning of the spring for the first time, April thirteenth, to be exact. You were returning from school with a friend. A couple of steps away, I heard her call you by your name.

"So you have been following me for the past six months?"

"Yes. I learned many things about you."

"Such as?" I was curious and yet I felt embarrassed in a way.

"Oh, very interesting things; I learned where you live. I know you have two younger sisters and a brother. The library is one of your favorite places. Your favorite color is beige and you like to feed birds. You are also crazy about that pair of shoes. Should I continue?"

"No, obviously I've been under the magnifying glass and didn't even realize it."

"Well, if you had known, then you wouldn't have acted as normally as you did. I wanted you to be you. I wanted to see what kind of person Fariba was."

"And you think that you know me now?"

"I didn't say that."

Why was I puzzled by what he said? "Somehow it feels uncomfortable to know this," I told him. "What happened to the whole privacy thing? Watching people without their knowledge is wrong."

Pooya was silent for a few seconds and then, "You're absolutely right. I'm very sorry and apologize if I offended you in any way. I didn't mean any harm, though. I just fell in love with you more and more each day and I wanted to know you."

I didn't answer him, so he continued, "Fariba, please forgive me. You may think of my act as an awful thing and you may be right. Can you find it in your heart to forgive me?"

*I paused and thought for a moment before I answered. "Yes."
And then I decided to drop that subject and not even think about
it. After all, I liked him and I had searched to see him for the past
month. I had looked at so many faces just to find his. I wasn't going
to drop him that easy. We continued to talk almost an hour before I
had to hang up when I heard the jingle of Papa's keys.*

*After that day, Pooya and I talked on the phone every little chance
we could get. I told Pooya not to call me at home. "Whenever it's safe,
I will call you myself," I told him. I didn't want to risk anything.*

*"Very well, I don't want to cause any trouble for you," he
agreed.*

*Through those phone conversations I learned many things about
him, too. Pooya, a first- born child of his middle class family was
twenty-three years old. His dad had worked as a librarian all his life
and his mom, a house- wife who dedicated her life to her children,
just like Mama. He had no brother, but a younger sister, name Shiva
whom he cherished, not only as a sister but also as his best friend and
a supporter whenever he needed one.*

*Of course the whole thing between Pooya and I had to remain
a secret. You know how it used to be in Iran in those days. I had to
hide everything about Pooya from my parents. Please don't take me
wrong. I loved my parents. They were good, hardworking, respectable
people who loved me. But in our Culture and Society, nothing could
be worse or more forbidden for a girl to have a boyfriend or to love a
boy. So I kept that a secret as long as I could.*

*Very soon we expanded our phone conversations to something even
better. We started to meet secretly. Pooya introduced me to his sister
Shiva when he brought her along in one of our hush-hush meetings.
Nineteen years old Shiva looked attractive and very feminine. Her
big Persian set of eyes shaped nicely with a black eyeliner which only
made their hazel color to stand out even more. Her skin seemed to
be smooth and lighter than Pooya's in color. I judged Shiva as kind
and affectionate and the test of time only proved my judgment. We
became the best of friends later on, and up until now we are still in
touch with each other.*

Pooya and I were good at meeting in public places to exchange love letters without attracting anyone's attention. At a time those letters became our only way of communication and I learned so much about him, his dreams and things he believed in. Through his writings, I found a sincere and unique person who became a dream come true for a girl like me. He filled my heart with beautiful things to dream on, and to live for.

Grandma Fariba got up and asked me to wait where I was. Then, she went to her bedroom. While waiting for her, my eyes explored the room. As long as I could remember, its warm atmosphere had always been welcoming. The walls were a serene, passive shade of blue. Her tall, exotic plants had always added that special touch of nature and beauty to every corner. I could remember the time I spent with and around her as a child and then as an adolescent; an era to cherish, which I did with all my heart.

A few minutes later, Grandma came back with a little treasure chest in her hand.

"This box carries the most valuable treasures of all. Through years with all the ups and downs in my life, this chest remained faithful and kept my treasures safe," she explained. Grandma opened the chest with a little golden key. Inside were all the letters Pooya had written for her.

"Passionately filled with emotions, his warm, tender words captured my heart. He took me away to a mysterious, and yet safe place every time I saw the twinkle in his eyes, or when his warm hands touched mine or when we exchanged letters.

"But there were also times when talking face-to-face, seemed impossible. Therefore, we allowed our eyes to speak the unspoken words. At times we couldn't see each other for days. All I had for comfort was hearing him on the phone or reading his letters as I imagined him there right next to me, close and personal."

Grandma sighed and then took a few papers out from the chest. She handed me some of those letters. "All the dark circles that you see on these papers are the footprints left by fallen tears.

The tears of vague sentiments and all the forlorn moments I spent without him." Her voice was rich with sorrow.

I looked over those papers. With time, their white color had turned yellow. Other than that, they were well kept not even a wrinkle on them. I could see the dark circles made by her tears on the papers. Holding the letters in my hands was mesmerizing. I felt a strong sense of energy, projecting from those papers. It made me shiver. Grandma noticed their effect on me and she smiled. For a while, she remained quiet as I searched through the letters.

"I like this one in particular. Pooya copied this from a book." Grandma pointed as she smiled and then handed the poem to me. "Why don't you read it for me?" Grandma asked.

I started to read aloud:

"I know for each drop of tear that falls on the ground,
A flower would grow and a butterfly would fly.
I know that our days are without sun,
And our nights has no star,
But I know at the end, it would be a light,
So I could build the cottage of our love,
I know that I would be in your heart,
And you would live forever, in mine,
then we would never be alone again.
Because I know for each tear that falls on the ground,
A flower would grow and a butterfly would fly."

When I finished reading that letter, I raised my head up and saw grandma's eyes; filled with tears, they mirrored the depth of her sorrow.

She sighed and then softly repeated, *"For each tear a flower will grow and a butterfly will fly.* This was Pooya's favorite. He copied and translated it from a poetry book he had. He told me who wrote it, but I can't remember the name of the poet now, not Persian. Pooya had a huge collection of international poems."

I couldn't let her continue her story. Tears danced in her eyes and I wanted to give her a moment to herself. To be honest, I felt like crying, too.

~

*W*e decided to call it a night. I couldn't believe how time flew. I helped with her usual bedtime routine. I cleaned the teapot and got it ready for the morning and placed the rest of fruits and pastries in the refrigerator. Grandma blew out all the candles and checked to see if all windows and doors were locked. When all was finished, I kissed her and wished her goodnight as I retired to the bedroom that used to be my mom's.

When I was younger, I slept in that room every time I stayed over at grandma's. As I laid down on the bed, I looked around. *"Everything is exactly the same way as your mother left it after she got married,"* Grandma had told me long ago. The maid who cleaned the house every Tuesday had strict orders: Everything dusted, washed or removed for cleaning, had to be placed back exactly as before. Sepideh's hair brush, her musical jewelry box on the wooden oak dresser, her five dolls on the shelf, and the big painting of three beautiful angels in paradise had always been a part of that room. The aqua color of the walls offered serenity and the light yellow curtains added color and brought harmony. *"Sepideh chose these colors when she was fifteen,"* I remembered grandma saying.

I stretched comfortably in bed and wrapped myself in freshly washed bed linens. I thought about Grandma and that boy, Pooya. *Who was he? And why had I never known he existed? Why had no one ever talked about him before?* Questions, questions and more questions continued to fill my head until a placid breeze from an open window started to run its invisible fingers gently in my hair. I surrendered and a deep sleep took me away.

~

$\mathcal{T}$he next day, soon after breakfast, Grandma and I went outside on her porch. Her Daffodils looked beautiful under the morning sun. We both sat on her wooden swing. "Sit here with me, for old days' sake," Grandma said. My memories ran far back to those afternoons when I used to stop by her house. I could always find Grandma by her little garden, sitting on the same swing bench, reading poems. Little by little, she taught me about the great Persian poets, such as Ferdosi and Hafez. They were the true Persian Poets in her eyes. *"When it comes to Persian literature, these are the names you should know about and be proud of,"* I remember her saying when I was only about ten years old.

Grandma took time to look at two yellow butterflies flying around the tops of her white lilies. Her love for nature had always amazed me. She watched as the butterflies flew away and then she started:

Despite the fear of being caught by our parents or our relatives, once in a while, Pooya and I walked hand in hand and carefree. We enjoyed those beautiful, unique moments. All seemed to be pure fun: the lies I had to tell to protect our little love affair, sneaking out and holding hands. All added excitement and thrill into our otherwise boring young lives. It kept us on our toes and we didn't mind. I can't tell you about the exhilaration of it all when I heard Pooya's secret whistle as he stood right under my window.

"We used to talk to each other for hours into the night. Those were the moments we both cherished. I remember leaving my window open at all times, especially at nights; I didn't want to miss his signal. My room's window on the second floor opened up to the street behind our house. It wasn't a thoroughfare but more like a narrow road alongside a recreational area. The fact that my parents never used the back road to get inside the house made our meetings possible. I felt so happy for not choosing the room on the opposite side, when we first moved in. Ferry ended up having that room. Her room faced the front street, the main entrance to our house.

"You asked me once why I always keep those wild thorny flowers in my bedroom, remember?" Grandma asked me.

"Yes, I remember asking you that. You said they're very special, but you never told me why."

"They're special because they became the symbol of our love."

"Symbol of your love! How?"

Grandma smiled.

One day, Pooya and I were supposed to meet at a valley near his house. I arrived earlier and as I waited for him, I saw those beautiful wildflowers, which I always liked but never tried to pick before. That day I thought it would be nice if I picked one for Pooya and gave it to him when he arrived. So I began to struggle with the thorny stem. I tried to pick the flower without injuring my fingers; a very hard task. I couldn't. It wasn't easy to cut its stem. "I need a knife." He arrived just as I finished thinking that thought. He approached me and said, "Allow me."

Then he picked the flower effortlessly, as if he never feared of injuring his fingers. He wrapped a handkerchief around its stem and handed it to me instead. Ever since, every time we saw that particular flower, he did the same. That's how it became the symbol of our love. I always keep them and cherish them just because they remind me of that particular day.

Pooya meant everything to me, everything I needed to feel alive; my mental nourishment, my emotional support. I needed him like a flower that needed sun to grow. I needed him as I needed air. I felt like a dry desert that had longed for a drop of rain. He became the rain, turned into a stream of love and ran through the desert of my heart. "You brightened up my whole world like a glistening golden sun," he always told me.

Grandma giggled again. I had to admit that I loved to see her laugh; it always made her look more beautiful. She continued:

As you know, the city of Esfahan is divided in half by Zayandeh River. The river separates the south from north and the historical "Khaju" bridge is one of the city's many overpasses that connects the two parts. Underneath "Khaju" on its lower level is a passage way made of large pebbles that leads into a little tea room. Right on top of that river, that little tea room became our favorite place to meet. Pooya and I used to sit on the benches inside and drink tea while we watched the flow of Zayandeh River beneath us.

We talked about our dreams and our future together. It felt so nice when I could comfortably lean my head on his strong shoulder and listen to him talk. At our favorite place on the river, we watched many colorful sunsets as well as many, many sunrises. My parents had so much trust in me that they never questioned my sudden interest for an early morning walk. Although I felt guilty for misusing their trust, the guilt never overpowered my love for Pooya and I continued to lie. Every morning I went to meet Pooya on the bridge and each day, hand in hand, we witnessed the beautiful dawn before he went to work.

He worked in the packaging center at a tobacco factory. With that kind of job, Pooya believed he would never stand a chance of asking my father for my hand in marriage. His job made him look inferior and that wasn't the way he wanted to be seen and judged by my father. He tried hard to find a more privileged job. Running into a dead end every time concerned him a great deal and made him worry. He told me so himself on the same day he talked about the war.

That morning at six o'clock, after getting ready for an allegedly early morning walk, I came down the stairs from my room. I saw Papa standing by the sofa, listening to the louder than usual radio in our living room. He had a serious look on his face. I heard him saying something to Mama about a war somewhere as she made breakfast in the kitchen. With only Pooya and our usual meeting in my thoughts, I didn't pay much attention to anything. I told them that I'm going for my morning walk. Come to think of it, they both seemed overly concerned about something. They didn't even hear me, or so it seemed. I rushed out of the house and hurried toward the bridge. Pooya was waiting for me. Strange! Everybody looked so serious, even Pooya.

"Why do you look worried?" I asked.

"Didn't you hear what happened this morning at four-thirty?"

"No, what happened?" I asked in a carefree way.

"Iraq has attacked one of our small villages near the borders."

"I overheard Papa as I rushed out to see you. He talked about the possibility of war and stuff like that, but I didn't stay to hear more."

"It's not a possibility anymore. The two countries declared war," he said. I didn't make any comment and remained quiet. I could see my composure surprised Pooya.

"So, how do you feel about it?" he asked.

"Well I feel bad for those people. But it's just by the border to the south, isn't it?" I really couldn't see the importance of it all at that point.

"Fariba, darling, There is something funny about war. It always spreads to the other parts and cities. Not only that, but it can also affect you and I in so many ways."

"In what ways; why should it affect us?"

"For one, it will be hopeless to find new employment and at the same time people may lose the jobs they already have."

"Why?" I asked him. To be honest, I didn't understand the connection between the war and occupation.

"Think about it, if the government's budget is low, how would they pay for costly weapons, machinery and all the other Army equipment? There would be lots of layoffs in order to balance the budget."

"But that's awful. People can't just lose their jobs," I objected.

"With the war, darling, jobs may not be the only thing they'll lose."

"So things may get worse?"

"Yes…But for now, let's just concentrate on one problem at a time."

"Our problem with Papa, you mean?" I asked.

"Yes. As we both discussed before, your dad wouldn't approve of me. He'll reject me. I've got to find a better job as soon as possible, before things get out of hand," he said.

I didn't make any comments and remained quiet. But I knew he was right. Papa would never agree for him to marry me. But how on Earth could Pooya find a better job? If what Pooya said was right, then the war just made things harder than they already were for us.

As a teacher, Papa believed in higher education. A college degree was a must-have condition for a future son-in-low. "Someone who's sophisticated and skilled would have a good paying job anyway. The key to wealth is education," Papa always argued.

Mama didn't care so much about an erudite son-in-law. She didn't believe that to be wealthy or to run a household always needed a college degree. "People with good businesses didn't all have degrees. As long as a man has a good heart and offers a well-managed life, I would have no objection," Mama used to say.

As a regular employee of the Tobacco Company, with a high school diploma, Pooya didn't meet any of my parents' expectations. His small salary couldn't support a family.

"What if I look for a job myself? That way we both can support each other. With two incomes we can build a good life for ourselves," I said joyfully. I could easily see his disagreement on the subject.

"That's absolutely out of the question," he burst with objection. "I'm sorry Fariba, but in my family no woman had to work in order to support the family. Both of our mothers never did. I'm not going to be less than our fathers."

"But, think about it, we…"

"Fariba, I said no, please. Look…even if I say it's okay for you to work, it's not going to make me look any better in your father's eyes anyway. I still would be the same guy working in a factory who's not able to provide for his family. As long as I'm not a professional or a rich person, I'll be nothing in his eyes and, therefore, unworthy of your love."

He made a point. Even if I could get a job to support my life, it wouldn't have changed Papa's point of view. It couldn't have changed how he would judge Pooya. Oh, what can I tell you? Sometimes I hated our culture and our society's beliefs. Why were things the way they were? Why couldn't I freely decide to whom I wanted to be married? I supposed, so many girls must have had thoughts like that and I wondered how many were able to actually marry the man they had loved. I couldn't possibly be the only girl who fell in love. Surely there were many like me, except no one ever talked about it. Why was it so bad to be a woman and work outside to help the family? Why couldn't I make Pooya and Papa understand that a woman could work and it didn't have to bring shame for men? Well, I couldn't change things that had been rooted deeply in our culture for centuries. I couldn't make anyone to understand my point of view. I felt as if I didn't belong to that era. I should have lived in a time when women had more freedom. Freedom to talk, freedom to love, and freedom to live the life they wanted.

"I felt trapped, trapped in a world that worked against all my beliefs." Grandma sighed and remained quiet for a few seconds, and then she said, "Things are so different now. You have your own career. You rule your own life. I'm glad things have changed, so that you and your children can live a better life."

Grandma was right; things had changed so much since then, people had changed. I could imagine how awful life must have been for a woman like grandma; a woman, so ahead of her time. I had noticed that about her a long time ago when, as a teenager, I could easily talk to her about my feelings. I could talk to her about anything and everything, while my other friends could never share their deepest thoughts with their grandmas. The way she understood my feelings connected us emotionally, more than I could say for my own mother. My mother was a good mom, but grandma had her own special place in my heart. In her, I saw a symbol of beauty, wisdom and humanity. I saw a woman of unlimited dreams, a goddess of peace whose heart was a sea of love. She couldn't be replaced and I felt so lucky having her as a grandmother.

As much as I wanted to hear her story, I couldn't help worrying about her well being. I paid close attention to her body language, looking for signs of fatigue.

"Grandma, do you want to rest a little?" I asked. She seemed a little tired. "I can make you a cup of tea?"

"No darling, I don't want tea, but I would like to rest."

"Then let me help you back to your room."

22

"What I would like to do is to sit here by my garden, on the swing, just a little longer," Grandma said with a smile.

"Of course, Grandma, tell you what? I'll go inside and start to write. You can take as much time as you need. We can continue with the rest of your story tomorrow. How is that?"

"Very well, you go ahead, I'll be in shortly," Grandma said.

I went to the dining room and sat at the table where I had my laptop and printer set up. From there, I could watch grandma through the window. Despite being an ocean of thoughts and mysteries, she looked collected and serene as she always did since I could remember. No matter what lies beneath, the surface of that ocean had always remained calm. I started to put my notes together. Grandma came inside soon after and the rest of the day we just enjoyed each other's company. We both went to bed early that night with a plan to continue the story first thing in the morning, right after breakfast.

The next morning, I couldn't wait to resume our expedition; Grandma seemed ready, too. After we finished breakfast we sat comfortably in her living room and she began:

With me out of high school, different families started to ask my father permission for my hand in marriage. Some asked for their sons, some wanted me to marry their brothers and there were those who just tried to be a match maker and introduce whole families together. Papa rejected them all. None of those people impressed him. 'But what if he did approve one of them?' God knew how many times I had asked myself that question and every time I felt a chill as I thought about the answer. The whole thing raised a great deal of concern. Time was so crucial at that point; I knew it would be soon before Papa would accept a family's proposal on my behalf. Pooya and I were running out of time and I, out of patience. The quicker I wanted Pooya to find a secure job, the slower the progress became.

We had our share of headaches and up and down moments when everything seemed so blurry and unclear. Stressed out by all the uncertainties, we had no choice but to pray for a miracle.

"How can we be together?" I asked him one day when Pooya and I went for a ride in town. "You know my father won't let me marry you." I was so distressed.

"Maybe not now, but if I find a good job, no, let me correct myself, when I find a good job, he will not have any objection."

"Well, obviously the good job isn't coming soon enough and it will only get worse with time and war; you told me that yourself."

He easily traced the anger in my voice. Pooya remained quiet as I continued, "We're running out of time. I finished high school and from now on people will come to ask my father for my hand in marriage. In fact, it's already started. I'm afraid one of those people will get his approval soon."

"Can't you just tell him you don't want to get married right now?"

"No, if he finds one of them good enough, he would make the decision himself, I won't have a say in that. You know how things are."

Pooya didn't answer. As he contemplated, I took advantage of his silence. "Why can't we just run away together?"

Shocked by my question, he said, "Fariba, I can't believe you just said that!" He held my hand. "You know that running away isn't the right solution."

"Then, tell me what is? Why do you have to do everything by the book?" I yelled.

Pooya sighed. He leaned back against the car seat. Was he angry? I couldn't say for sure. But I could read the disappointment all over him; disappointed for not being rich, for not being a successful businessman. Immediately I regretted yelling at him. 'I shouldn't have told him about those people asking for my hand in marriage,' I thought remorsefully. I didn't want to make him worry. I felt his emotional pain and saw the look of despair in his young face. I hugged him and told him not to feel sad. I told him that he was my perfect man and no matter what, I would find a way to wait for him.

"Oh, Pooya I love you so much, I will love you forever. Don't worry about anything, nothing at all. You are my destiny, don't you know?"

He held my arms and pulled me close, looked deeply into my eyes for a few seconds before he fastened my lips with a passionate, loving kiss for the first time. It felt as if a strong current of electricity passed through my whole body and traveled through each and every cell. He kissed me over and over. His lips traveled down my neck, then toward my shoulders and moved up again. My heart began to beat faster as his hand gently caressed my breasts. Suddenly I pulled back and held his hand; my virgin body and mind rejected the touch at first, but when he bent a little and his feverish lips landed softly on my lips again; I knew that I wasn't going to stop him no matter how far he wanted to go. I had never felt like that before. I wanted to belong to him. I wanted him so much.

Despite the cold February night, my whole body burned like a torch. Our body heat steamed up the car's windows, and made a thin shield between us and the outside world. I didn't want to move, I couldn't move. Our little inner world, so perfect, so subtle and safe couldn't be touched. Every inch of my body longed for him. I didn't care about consequences. I had no objection to committing the most sinful crime a Muslim girl in Iran could commit by giving herself to a man who was not her husband. But for the man that he was, it didn't get any further than a kiss; he stopped.

"I'm going to regret this," he said.

"Why? Why Pooya? I want to be yours," I pleaded.

"You are mine, my love. But we should do things the right way. I should not take advantage of you here, not this way; this is wrong. I will never forgive myself for that."

Quiet and confused, I felt disappointed. Did he have to be such a gentleman? Why did everything have to be done the right way?

That night I returned home with a pretend headache and went to bed early. However, I couldn't sleep at all. Burning with desire, my body yearned for his touch.

Chapter 2

I remember the night of March 18th. I woke up in the middle of
the night by the most horrible sound of an explosion, which was
immediately followed by a few more blasts.

"Mama! Papa!" I screamed as I sat in my bed, confused and
scared. My legs felt numb by the fear. Papa opened the door and
entered my room a few seconds later.

"Hurry up, run to the basement," he shouted.

"What's going on? What was that?" I questioned with panic.

"Just run to the basement," he said again as he rushed to Zina's
room. Soon he came back out, carrying Zina. When he saw me still
standing in shock, he put one of his hands on my back, and gave me
a push. "Come on, let's go," he yelled.

As we started to run down the stairs, nearby blasts shocked our
house and I almost fell down, but managed to hold my balance. Papa
held on to Zina with one hand and with the other, tried to grab me.

The paintings on the wall near the staircase fell down; somewhere else I heard glasses shattering. 'We can never make it to the basement,' I thought with fear, but we did make it. There, in the basement I saw Mama, holding Ferry and Zafa as close as she could. There were loud noises outside. The sound of the red alarm* blared loud and clear. I knew we were being attacked by the Iraqi air force, but up until that night, the war had only affected certain parts of the country. The cities in the south and the southwest by the borders of the two countries were hit day after day. We used to watch the broadcast on TV every night, and each time I asked myself how people could endure such things. I felt happy that we didn't have to go through those horrible events. Since the beginning of the war Esfahan had suffered from economical hardship but not from any air attacks. Childishly, I thought being far from south was what kept us safe; obviously, I was wrong.

My family and I sat in our basement in a circle and held each other's hands helplessly. I could hear the engines of the airplanes as they flew over our house and passed us by. Then suddenly, I couldn't hear the engines anymore. Instantly, a loud silence took over. You know what I mean by a loud silence? I mean when the silence is bothering your ears. When the silence is the last thing you want to hear. When the silence makes you scared, and you would wonder what's going to happen. When you know that something more fearsome would break the silence anytime. The most dreadful moment of stillness I had ever experienced, just like the calm in the center of a storm. I could hear my own heartbeat, waiting, waiting for horror to start again and it did. The hideous sound of falling bombs, whistling as they ripped through the air broke the silence. Then, there were the hits and blasts that followed again and again. Windows were shattered; pieces of glass flew in the air.

I could hear the people screaming in between the loud sirens of the ambulances. Zafa and Zina's continuous cries didn't help me stay

---

* Red alarm – The alarms were color-coded. Red alarm meant possibility/ or start of an air attack and it also meant to seek shelters. White alarm meant that the air attack had ended and it was safe for civilians to come out of their hiding places.

calm. They hid themselves in Mama's arms. Although shaking, Ferry seemed unusually quiet. Papa's arms invited Ferry and me. He tried his best to protect us by using his body as a shield. Praying aloud, poor Mama kept on sending prayers of protection for each one of us.

A few minutes later, we heard the alarm again. Radio indicated the color "white" this time, Iraqi jets had left our sky and we were safe. We went outside to look at what had become of our town. Without electricity, the city remained in the dark for the next half an hour. Illuminations from the explosions were the only source of light we had. Heavy smoke in the air burned my eyes and made breathing somewhat difficult. I couldn't remember being scared like that in my life ever before. I remember that first night of air attack in detail. The memory of it has never left me.

I couldn't believe what had just happened. I looked at my family to ask, was it real, or was it a dream? But when I saw the shock in their eyes, I knew. I saw a horrible reality, far from any dream. For the first time, we experienced how it felt to be touched by the evil claws of war and the ugliness of it all. I couldn't believe that what I used to see only in movies had just happened in my own real life. I cannot describe how I felt that day. My beautiful inner world had been shattered and hung upside down. Fearful and worried, I thought about all the people I loved, Mama, Papa, my sisters and brother, relatives, friends, and Pooya…. Oh God, Pooya! Was he okay?

"Where did the bomb hit? Which house? Which building? Papa, where did those bombs hit?" I kept asking Papa intolerantly.

"I don't know yet, darling. We will know soon," he answered. I traced distress in his voice, too, even though he tried to act calm.

"Don't worry, Fariba. I'm sure our friends and relatives are all fine," Mama said.

'How can she be sure?' I asked myself as I looked at her. How is it possible for anyone not to worry? I wanted to scream at Mama and tell her, "Stop treating me like a child. I want you to tell me the truth and the truth is that we don't know whether or not our relatives and friends are okay. So please don't tell me not to be scared or concerned." War wasn't a small booboo that Mama could just kiss it away and

make it all better for me. But, of course, I didn't say a word. I knew Mama didn't mean any harm. I preferred Papa's realistic response when he said he didn't know where the bombs hit.

Understandably, I felt upset. First of all, I had witnessed something ugly and horrific and second of all, I didn't know how Pooya was. Not knowing, was a trigger that any wrong answer could pull to hit my insanity. Papa told us to get back in the house. He said he was going to check the neighbors. When I went back upstairs, I tried to call Pooya, but the phone line wasn't working. Two hours of dilemma had passed and still no news about my Pooya; it seemed like eternity. It was almost near dawn and Papa hadn't returned home yet. Still in shock by the whole event, I heard red alarm piercing through the city once more. "Not again, not again!" I screamed. We ran to seek shelter. This time I cried aloud, I couldn't take it and I broke down. Mama tried to assure me that we were going to be safe in the basement. But I wasn't listening. "Why didn't Papa come back? Where is he? … where is he?" I cried.

I could hear the whistles of each bomb as they fell on the city and every time I felt hatred toward the pilot, the murderer, the evil man behind the wheel of those jets, the hand that pushed a button to kill us all. Why did he want to kill us? What did we do to him? I couldn't understand at first, but then I realized it wasn't anything personal. War simply meant that; it meant the end of humanity where people killed one another without even knowing who they killed and why. I shivered, I cried, and looked at Mama's face and my siblings. I didn't want any of them to get hurt. I worried about Papa and about Pooya, too.

A few minutes later, the basement door opened and someone rushed in.

"Papa!" I jumped to say.

"Are you all okay?" he asked as he ran to us.

"Yes, we are," Mama answered.

"It's bad out there. A few blocks down, houses are destroyed and lots of people are injured," Papa told Mama quietly, but I heard him.

Were those the last moments we had together? What about the next bomb, or the one after that? Which one would hit us? I thought of those questions every time I heard the whistle of a bomb falling, as it ripped through the air, as it sounded right above our house, coming down on us. And every time, with each distant explosion, I felt relief, because I knew it hadn't hit our house, but somebody else's. 'It is selfish to feel relieved!' my guilty conscience yelled, but I couldn't change how I felt. It always felt good to be alive for the first few seconds after each hit. Right before feeling severe anxiety as I started to think about all the people I knew; the relatives and friends from school, neighbors and even Mr. Mofid, the owner of that little deli at the corner.

Well, we survived the night. Pooya and his family did, too. After that, we had to take one day at a time. We had to stay alive day by day and not think about tomorrows. What could tomorrow bring, Death? Or could it bring peace again? I asked myself and didn't know the answer, nobody knew; we couldn't plan anything. Everything remained on hold, our lives, our vivacity and exuberance. We just hoped that tomorrow would bring humanity back and the countries would stop the war.

Needless to say, the "tomorrow" we all hoped for, brought only the same thing, more war. Air attacks continued each day and every single night. By then, I had no choice but to accept it as a way of life. I had to live and move on no matter what, and I did. Up to this very moment, I can still hear the whistle of the falling bombs in my head. I still jump with fear, by the sound of every thunder clap or the glow of every lightning strike.

Those days when "War" was dancing his way into every corner of our city, my love affair with Pooya kept me alive emotionally. Pooya and I grew in love a little more each day and it felt very good. When we were together, our love took us faraway to a place where "peace" lived; a beautiful, resting place with no heartache. But then again we had to return back to reality and the ugliness that came with it. The evil, we could feel and see its presence in our daily lives.

So many new laws were made and came in effect as the result of the war and one of the latest edicts worsened our situation. 'Any man under thirty years of age was not allowed to attend college or seek employments unless he served in the army first,' the new law ruled. "A hard thing just became impossible now," I told Pooya with despair." 'How on Earth could he get another job?' He didn't say it, but I'm pretty sure he thought it at that moment.

Eight more months had passed since the first attack. By November, our bleeding country seemed vulnerable. Iran had lost men at the borders in South. The death tolls for Iranian soldiers were enormously high. Iran needed help and no other country offered any. The sanction by America added to the problems, too. Shortage of narcotics and medications, such as pain- killers, anesthetics and antibiotics made things worse.

Most nights we didn't have electricity. The people in charge shut down power either to preserve supplies or to protect the city from the air attacks. Standing up on its own feet, Iran had suffered a great deal. People endured so much pain and misery in every way possible. Lives were lost every day and night. Economically, everything cost twice as much or more. It seemed the only thing that had no value was Life, itself.

~

A year and a half had passed since Pooya and I met. In March, trees had blossomed already. Far from our houses in a most beautiful place called 'grassland', Pooya and I were walking. Everything seemed to be peaceful. People all around us looked calm and happy; away from the reality of their lives, whatever that might have been. Some people were walking as couples and some were alone.

"I forgot how beautiful the world is," I said.

"The way things have been, who can remember?"

"I would give anything for time to stop right at this minute and stay this way until the end."

"You mean we walk here in this meadow until the end?" he asked jokingly.

"No silly. I meant—"

He interrupted me with a warm kiss. "I know what you mean, darling. I wish it, too."

"What do you think will happen to us?" I asked.

"I don't know and sometimes I don't want to think about it. Let's enjoy the moment for now." He put his arm around my shoulder and pulled me closer. I leaned my head on his shoulder. It felt good and safe. "I love you, Pooya, I love you very much."

"Me too, my love, you're the rainbow of my world."

"You know how I love it when you talk to me like that. Tell me more," I demanded with a smile.

"You brought colors into my black and white existence, you—"

"What was that? Did you hear it?" I interrupted him fearfully.

"I heard it, it sounded like machine guns. It's coming from there..." he said as we both turned toward the noise. Right on our left, we saw a large group of people running down the hill and toward us. For a few seconds, we didn't know exactly what was going on. We didn't move; it was as if we were frozen until we saw an Iraqi plane. The plane flew at a very low altitude, opening fire on people with its large machine guns.

We both started to run, just to be out of the site, to find shelter. But what kind of a shelter could one find in a meadow? It was a big group of people with nowhere to hide. People were falling down all around us on the ground, like flies. At first, the sound of their screams and the guns was all I could hear, but soon, as I kept running, it all started to fade away. Before long, those sounds were just fuzzy echoes in the background of my own heartbeat, which became louder and stronger and began to bother me. The only sound that proved I was alive became a harsh music to my inner ears.

I felt the faster I tried to run, the slower my steps became, as if I ran in slow motion to hide from the furious bullets of the roaring enemy. Pooya held onto my hand and I tried to catch up to his speed. I noticed a young girl on my left. She ran almost at the same pace we did. The girl and I looked at each other for maybe less than a second as we continued to run. We could hear the engines of the plane right behind us.

"Lie down. Stop running, lie down. Lie down!" Pooya yelled to everyone around. I could hear him clearly. Unlike all the other noises in my ear, his voice wasn't fuzzy at all. Next thing I knew, he pushed me down. I realized some people followed his advice and some didn't and continued to run. The girl beside me didn't stop. Pooya and I dropped ourselves on the ground. I put my arms around my head with my face down. I closed my eyes as a chain of roaring bullets drew a long line on the ground beside me.

The whole event took maybe less than two minutes. When the plane flew by, I opened my eyes. First thing I did, I turned my head to my right to look at Pooya. He seemed okay. Then I looked around. The next thing I saw was the body of that young girl a few steps away. Her eyes were open with a stare that looked right at me, just as my eyes were locked on her lifeless body and her innocent face. I looked into her youthful, yet spark-less eyes. They had no trace of subsistence, or hope. Her life had ended in a matter of seconds with all the dreams she might have had; all buried in the cemetery of her young heart. I sat there on the same spot and wept. I cried for the girl, for the nameless face. But I knew her face would live on in my memory forever. I kept thinking, 'Who was she? What were her dreams? Was she in love with someone? Did somebody love her?'

Pooya tried to console and comfort me, but the trauma of that moment hit me strong. I couldn't stop shivering as tears covered my face. I cried in silence. Soon he gave up his pointless effort and he, too, sat next to me quietly. A deep sorrow took over our existence while we held hands and watched the bodies of innocents.

And of course, life went on day after day; it had to. We had to.

~

*A*s Pooya once predicted, big companies as well as small businesses started to lay off employees. In jobless families, escalated fears only added more misery to their lives. As for the rest of the people still with jobs, the scenery didn't seem prettier. Lack of security, uncertainty and despair entered everyone's heart and touched every *household in its own way. I knew that my parents were concerned and worried about our well being, not only for that particular time, but also for our future. Considering all the things going on, I knew Papa would think twice before saying "no" to people who asked him about my hand in marriage. Iran's economic status made anyone with an established business in hand, a good candidate for a son-in-law. At that point, having a high education was secondary compared to wealth. Before the war, a college degree was a must, according to Papa. But at that particular period, he began to accept Mama's point of view. "A promised, well-managed life for my daughters is good enough," Mama used to say and Papa couldn't argue any longer, not when everything he dreamed of for the future seemed lost. Strangely, things were changing. People had changed; their ideas, their goals and the way everybody looked at life.*

～

*O*ne autumn afternoon, someone rang our doorbell. We had just finished eating lunch. I opened the door and saw Bibi with a big grin on her face. She was an old lady who earned her living by cleaning people's houses. As a maid, she knew almost everybody's personal life in detail. She also loved to introduce families for matrimonial purposes. People knew her as a matchmaker and usually sent her for those missions. She worked for Mama every once in a while; mostly around our New Year, when Mama cleaned and literally washed our house from top to bottom. It surprised me to see Bibi early in the afternoon in our house when Mama hadn't called for her services. I felt very uncomfortable by her presence. 'What on earth did she want to tell Mama?' The question danced in my head.*

"Bibi! What a nice surprise," Mama said as she came to the door.

"Hello Mrs. Abari, I came to talk to you about a very pleasant matter."

"Well, nothing is better than a happy talk. Come on in, Bibi." Mama smiled as she moved aside to let her in.

Bibi followed Mama into the kitchen with slow steps. All the extra weight she carried made walking seems like a hard task. I followed them both. They sat at the table.

"Bibi would you like to eat something?"

"No, Mrs. Abari, thank you. I just ate at Miss Shamsi's house."

"Fariba, why don't you bring some tea for us?" Mama asked. A few minutes later, I brought tea to the table and sat next to Mama as Bibi spoke.

"I worked for Miss Shamsi today," Bibi said. "I don't think you know her family. They're very nice, respectable people. They also have a son who is thirty- three years old. He goes to college. They are a decent family, Mrs. Abari." Bibi stopped talking and stared into Mama's eyes, waiting for Mama to respond and Mama did.

"Bibi, why are you telling me about this family?"

"I'll get to that right now. They are looking for a wife for their son. They asked me if I knew a nice girl around here. I said of course I do. I told them about your daughter. Now they want to see your daughter, of course with your permission," she explained and my heart dropped.

"Mama, I don't want to get married now." I jumped in the middle of their conversation to protest.

Mama's right eyebrow went upward as she looked at me. I knew what that look meant. It meant I shouldn't interfere. Furious wasn't a good enough word to explain how I felt at that moment. 'Why did Bibi have to find a husband for me?' I thought with anger. Oh, I wanted to scream, but of course I didn't.

"As you know, Bibi, I can't tell you anything unless I talk to my husband first."

"Of course, I know that…." Bibi paused to think about something and then she added: "Even if Miss Fariba doesn't want him, maybe her sister Miss Ferry would?"

"Ferry?….. She's still too young Bibi. Anyhow we can't let people come for Ferry's hand in marriage while Fariba is still in our house unmarried."

"*I don't mind.*" *I ran in their conversation again.* "*I mean, I don't mind if Ferry marries before me.*" *I said, hoping Mama would accept my generous offer of stepping out as an older sister for Ferry's sake.*

"*Fariba, you stay out of this. As long as you're not married, none of your sisters are going to get married.*"

"*But why not?*"

"*It doesn't look good in people's eyes if your younger sister finds a husband before you.*"

"*That's so silly.*" *I didn't know whether I should laugh or cry at that rule.*

"*It's been like this all along Fariba. This is part of our tradition. The first daughter has to marry before the next.*"

"*What if I never get married, then what? My sisters have to remain at home and without a husband just because I didn't want to marry?*" *I couldn't understand the reasoning behind it.*

"*Well, I'm glad that's not the case and you'll get married,*" *Mama said smiling.*

"*But Mama…*"

"*Fariba, be quiet please*" *Mama ordered. Then she turned to Bibi.* "*Bibi, like I said, I will talk to my husband and let you know. If he agrees, then we set up a meeting with them. I'm sure my husband would like to sit with them and ask some questions.*"

"*Yes Mrs. Abari.*" *Bibi said with smile.* "*I will wait for your answer before I say anything to them.*" *She added while her eyes searched the walls for a clock.* "*My goodness, what time is it now?*" *BiBi asked, but before Mama could answer, she added,* "*I better go now.*" *Bibi got up.* "*Please forgive me for taking so much of your time.*"

"*It's all right Bibi. Thank you for coming.*"

We followed Bibi to the door. Just before stepping out, she said, "*I almost forgot, I didn't mention their family name. His father's name is Mr. Ali Hekmat and the boy's name is Morad.*"

After giving that last bit of information, Bibi left. I saw Mama memorizing those names. At that point, I wanted Miss Shamsi and her family to disappear from the face of the Earth. '*I hope Papa*

*disapproves of them just like he has eliminated all the others so far.'
I wished while thinking about Miss Shamsi's family, analyzing their
plusses and minuses in my head to determine Papa's answer. Their
son had some college education. They were rich, too, since they could
afford a maid. Having a maid at that time was certainly a luxury.
Those were the plusses, but what were the minuses? I couldn't think
of any. Thoughts ran through my brain like shooting stars.*

*The whole thing worried me to death. I hated Bibi for coming to
our house that afternoon. I hated Miss Shamsi and her family. Wasn't
that funny? I hated people I hadn't even met yet.*

*I thought about Miss Shamsi's family until I felt sick to my
stomach. Papa wasn't home yet. I couldn't wait any longer. I had to
know what he would say.*

*The day dragged itself as long as it could. Every minute seemed
like an eternity. I stayed in my room and waited. Finally, Papa came
home. Mama didn't say anything over dinner. Perhaps she didn't
want to talk about it in front of Ferry, Zina or Zafa. I waited again.
I hate to wait, I always did.*

*Finally, after the dinner, the other children went to the living
room to watch television. I offered to wash the dishes so I could stay
in the kitchen while they talked, confident that Mama would bring
up the subject soon. Well, she did.*

"Bibi came here today. She found a husband for Fariba."

*I wished Mama would stop saying that. 'Bibi found a husband,'
I mimicked her in my head. 'He was not my husband and he wasn't
going to be.' I thought with anger.*

"Oh…who is he?" Papa asked.

"He is the son of Mr. and Mrs. Hekmat."

"Hekmat? …Ali Hekmat?"

*"Yes, actually Bibi said Ali Hekmat is his father and the boy's
name is Morad."*

I withheld my breath while I waited for his answer.

*"Oh no, …no." Papa laughed while Mama and I both stared at
him. I took a big breath and swallowed some air. Did I hear right?
He said "no"!*

"Why not? Atta, why are you laughing? I think they're a good family. Their son is in college and obviously they're not poor," Mama enlightened him.

"I went to high school with Ali Hekmat," Papa explained. *"He and I are not on good terms with each other. Perhaps Bibi hadn't mentioned our name to that family yet. Otherwise, he would never dare to ask such a thing."* Papa got up from the table and walked toward the living room as he continued to talk.

"Over my dead body; asking for my daughter's hand in marriage?" Papa started to laugh again. I still could hear him laugh as he sat on the living room sofa. God had given me a second life, that's how it felt. Much easier than I thought it would be, I didn't have to do anything. Papa turned them down without any hesitation. 'Perfect,' I thought.

I didn't withhold my breath anymore. So far, God supported Pooya and me. With God on our side, I felt happy and only one question remained in my head: How to find a good job for Pooya as fast as possible? I knew Pooya had zero to a very little chance of getting hired, not after the new law. In order to get hired anywhere, he needed to serve in the army for two years. Business men didn't want to risk anything by hiring a young man who hadn't served yet and that meant risking everything they had. They could lose their businesses as well as serve time in jail if someone reported them for disobeying that law by hiring men like Pooya. It seemed like a dead end street. 'So forget about finding a job,' I thought.

On the other hand, how could I go through all that misery every time someone rang our bell? I could of course just work on the idea of a husband for Ferry first. That didn't seem like a bad plan. Only if I could talk to Mama and change her mind about that crazy tradition she talked about. 'Just because she gave birth to me first, I have to marry before my other sisters? Talk about first come, first served,' I thought with mockery. I needed them to believe that I seriously didn't want to get married. Maybe then, they could forget about me and start concentrating on Ferry. I remember that night I didn't sleep; the *whole night I planned about how to push my sister toward marriage before me. Poor Ferry.*

⁓

*S*pring *arrived again and filled the air with the scent of blossom trees. The light, fresh air felt pleasant and my lungs couldn't get enough of it. With no air attack for the last few days, our city looked peaceful. It almost made the whole war seems like a bad dream and not a reality. An early morning rain made the streets shiny and fresh. The smell of newly cut grass delightfully wrapped itself in the air. Papa always scattered some new seeds in the middle of March in our backyard. The moderate temperature made the grass grow fast. In mid April, it already needed to be trimmed and Papa always made the grass look neat. It was a calm day, I can recall, and I had spent awhile in our garden. Mama's daffodils looked great, so I cut a few yellows and a couple of whites for my room. In the kitchen, I found my favorite vase that had seemed to be missing for a while; I found it in one of the cabinets.*

I started to arrange the flowers in the vase when Ferry asked, "Papa, what's going on? There are so many cars parked outside and one of them is blocking our driveway."

"Those cars belong to our neighbor's relatives and friends," Papa said with calm and continued to read the newspaper.

"Which neighbor?" I asked.

"The Monirans," Mama said as she added the sauce into the pot of meat.

"They have another party perhaps," I told Ferry carelessly.

"No darling." Papa said. "Their son is going to the south. He's going to be a soldier. Their relatives are coming to see him and wish him well before he leaves."

"What? You mean that clumsy seventeen year old is going to war? He can't even dress himself yet," I laughed. To me, the whole idea seemed like a joke.

"Fariba it's not nice to talk about him like that. It's very insensitive of you. You should be ashamed of yourself." Mama's right eyebrow was pulled upward as she looked at me.

"But Mama, you remember Mrs. Moniran said she would never let her son go to war? It was just last week when she said all that, she gave us an hour speech about her not believing in the cause."

"Yes, I remember what she told us last week. But a lot has changed since then." Mama seemed serious.

"What has changed? I can't believe the Army accepted him? What can that gangly boy possibly do for the Army? I can't believe they want him." I laughed again.

"Well, Fariba, if you listen to the news a little, you would know what is going on in our country. Our Army is asking for help. They have a new law in effect as of yesterday."

"What new law?" Ferry asked.

"Every young man below the age of thirty has to report to the Army within a week." Mama explained.

"What?... A draft? Did she say in a week?" I jumped. *That couldn't be. That couldn't be true.* Mama started to explain the news to us, but I didn't listen much. My mind traveled far, far away. I had to talk to Pooya and check for the accuracy of what Mama had just said; hoping to hear him say, *"No, it isn't true."* I ran upstairs, called Pooya and asked him to meet me on the bridge. As soon as he arrived I asked him about the draft.

"Yes my darling, it's a draft. Every man below thirty and over sixteen has to register and leave within a week. They need men in South."

"Oh no, please God, no." I think my whole body froze, it certainly felt that way. Deep inside myself I wanted to scream, weep and yell. But I remained quiet. At twenty-six, Pooya qualified. That particular law had put him right in the middle of the chosen category. *'That means he has to leave in a week,'* I thought and realized in fear.

"Is there any way out of this? Is there any way at all for you to stay and not register?" I asked doubtingly.

40

"No, I'm afraid not. They actually came to our house last night and asked about me."

"What? Who came to your house?"

"You know who; the Army Police. Their job is to find young men and report them to the Army."

"Wait a minute; they just made this new law! How come they came to your house last night?" I asked, but didn't wait for him to answer. *"I don't understand this, it seems as if they stood by your door and jumped in as soon as they issued the law."* I added as a joke. But no one laughed, not even me.

"They made the law yesterday morning darling. By night, they had registered hundreds of men already."

"So then, when are you leaving?" Immediately I regretted asking the question,' I wished I had never asked. I wished I could take it back; I didn't want him to answer that, but he did.

"I leave in two days, that is—"

"In two days?" I interrupted him to ask in terror. *"What do you mean in two days?"*

"I'm trying to tell you. That's how they scheduled me."

"But, but what about us, what will happen to us?" I cried.

"Fariba, listen to me." He held both my wrists as he started to talk. *"I'll be back, I promise."* He kissed me on the forehead and wiped my tears away with his cold fingers.

"Please don't cry, Fariba. Watching you cry makes my heart ache."

Despite what he had told me, my tears rushed down. I never knew I had that many tears to spare.

Pooya kept talking to me, *"You have to be strong, Fariba. Be strong for me and I'll be strong for you. I need to know that you will be okay and then I'll be fine."*

"I'll be strong," I told him; I tried to swallow the big, painful knot in my throat. *"I just need a moment, Pooya."* My forehead rested on his chest as I kept a tight grip of his sleeves to keep him close. His arms wrapped around me and pulled me closer. He kissed me again and

softly tucked in a few strands of uncovered hair that hanged down from the corner of my veil.

He said that he would come to see me, to say good-bye before he left and then I cried as he walked away. When he reached the first block, I saw him wiping something away from his face. I think he cried too.

Finally, the day I feared the most had arrived. Pooya said he wanted to come to see me and to say goodbye. Upstairs, at eight thirty in the evening, I waited in my room, listening for his special whistle to sneak out and meet him in the street behind the house. He hadn't arrived yet and anxiety began to crawl under my skin. Crazy thoughts started to march inside my head. I kept watching the clock; the clicking sound of it bothered me as it moved forward with slow steps and every minute hammered my nerves as it passed. I couldn't wait any longer. I had just gotten up to call him, when I heard his whistle. 'Finally,' I thought as I grabbed the letter that I'd written for him earlier and stuck it in my pocket as I ran toward the stairs. Just when I reached the second step, the power went off without warning and everywhere became unexpectedly dark. I couldn't see a thing. The electric outage was followed by the sound of red alarm. Everything happened so fast, my eyes needed time to adjust to the sudden darkness. I tried to hold onto the side rails for a moment. Seemingly a second later, I heard an explosion that shocked our house so strongly I lost my balance and fell down the stairs.

I don't remember much after the fall, except that I woke up a few hours later in the hospital. Apart from some minor bruises, I didn't have serious injuries. But because of the fact that I lost consciousness, the doctor wanted to keep me there for observation.

When I realized what had happened I wanted to die. How could God be that cruel and let this happen? How could God let my dear Pooya leave without me seeing him? I needed to see him. I wanted to give him my letter. I wanted to kiss him, to say goodbye and wish him well. He must have gone to the south by then. I knew that Pooya could never guess what had happened to me and why I hadn't stepped out to see him. Under my window in that dark street behind the house, he must have waited for me to show up as we planned. He could have never guessed in a million years that my parents had rushed me to the hospital.

Grandma stopped talking. Saddened by the memories, she turned her head away, but I already saw the tears that shined in her eyes like the blink of a star. She composed herself and started again:

The doctor discharged me from the hospital the next day. In my pocket, exactly where I had left it, I found the letter I wrote for Pooya. 'Thank God no one had seen it in my pocket,' I thought as I dialed Shiva's number.

Happy to hear her voice I asked about Pooya.

"They took him last night," she told me.

"Where?....Which city? Which part of the south?"

"They didn't tell us anything about where he was going to be," she said.

"You didn't ask?"

"Of course we did, but they said we have to wait until he gets there and then he will call to let us know where he is."

"What nonsense! How can they do this? Why couldn't they say?" I asked with anger.

"Fariba, you know they do what they want. We just have to wait."

"Did he say anything about me?" I asked Shiva impatiently.

"He didn't get a chance to talk to me alone much. He returned home very late. A soldier who had been waiting for him at our house agreed to give Pooya another half an hour as Pooya requested. He went to his room and wrote a letter for you. He made me promise to deliver it as soon as possible." Shiva explained.

I couldn't wait to read his letter. That afternoon Shiva came to our house. I hugged her, I knew her pain. we both loved Pooya and didn't want him to be out there in a place where humanity was long gone. Shiva handed me a sealed envelope as she sat beside me and then we talked for a while. I didn't insist on keeping Shiva there with me any longer than she wanted to stay. When she left I ran back to my room and opened the envelope. My wobbly hands could hardly hold the paper steady. In his letter Pooya wrote:

"My dear Fariba, my angel,
I don't know what happened and why you didn't Come out to see me. Whatever the reason might have been,
I'm sure it was something you couldn't help or change, otherwise I know you would have. Because your kind heart must have known How painful it would be for me to leave without seeing you.
My beloved, my Fariba,
Not being able to see you made my heart weep. The tears that ran down my face on my way back home poured from the depths of my heart. I'm in pain, for I have already missed you.
Tonight when I reached the street in the back,
I whistled and waited under your window.
First the electricity went out and then I heard the red alarm.
Probably you had to go to the basement with the rest of your family. Anyway, I didn't want you to come out at that point. I wanted you to be safe first.
I looked for a secure place myself. I went inside the canal near your house and I took shelter there until the attack was over.
Then I came back under your window and whistled again.
I waited three hours. I walked up and down, but you never showed up. I worried and grew impatient.
Once or twice a thought came to my head to ring your doorbell and ask for you.
For a moment, I didn't care if I had to face your father or what he would do to me.
But when I thought about the problem it could cause you, especially at the time when I wasn't going to be around, I decided not to ring.
Finally I had to go back home. I'm sad and my heart is broken. Where were you my love?

It is now half past midnight. A soldier is waiting for me in our living room to take me to the airport. I have to leave now. I will let you know where I'll be as soon as I find that out myself.

My beautiful Fariba, I have carved the image of you In my heart, which I'm going to take with me; this way You'll be always near, in my heart, in my thoughts and everywhere I go. Don't worry my love. We'll be fine.

With love,
Pooya

God knows how many times I have read that letter and how many tears I have shed every time. He was gone and I couldn't do anything about it. I wished that I could bring back and recreate that night the way it was meant to be; to stay in his arms and hold him tight. To tell him how much I loved him and needed him.

Chapter 3

*A*fter almost two weeks since Pooya left, Shiva and her family still didn't know exactly where they had taken him. "Where is he?" I kept on asking and the question remained unanswered. I prayed each day and every night as my concerns for him increased. Afraid for his life, I asked God not to let them send him to the front line.

People were told that all these young men were taken to a training facility for only two weeks where they could learn about the basic principles of war and also about military hardware. After that, they were sent to the borders and all they needed to know was how to use their weapons. Nothing else mattered, "just follow the orders and obey the rules. Kill or be killed, shoot the enemy before they shoot you;" and those, were the rules.

Seventeen days had passed and according that assumption about training period, Pooya's two weeks of preparation had finished. "But where had they send him to?" We wanted to know. I called Shiva every single day to find out if she knew anything. Finally in the third week Shiva told me they had received a call from him. She said he couldn't stay on the phone for long and he only spoke briefly to his mother.

"They had ordered him to stay in the south's biggest city "Abadan" for a while." Shiva explained.

"The borders and the front line are far from where I am posted, don't worry." He had told his mother.

I felt relieved; alas short lived, my composure came to an end when about two months later his family had received another call from him with a news no one wanted to hear.

"They are going to sent him to the border in two days." Shiva told me and my nightmare came to life.

"No, they can't do that, they can't send him there!" I almost screamed. "He doesn't have enough training."

"What can we do except to pray?" Shiva asked. Then added, "Every day, my mother goes to the house of worship to pray, she lights a candle for Pooya and all the other soldiers." Her voice didn't sound much better than mine; the voice of anguish. I realized and I painfully admitted we couldn't change anything, no matter how much we wanted to.

Still under attack, our city continued to suffer the consequences. Exhausted from all the misery war brought us, everyone seemed embittered. The war left people irritated; they were emotionally wounded, also economically broken. Almost every family had lost someone either in the south or in our own city during the air attacks. Lives were lost and shattered. The casualties of the war had risen. We lost some relatives, too, and no matter how many deaths we saw, the news always managed to shock us tragically when reporting the death of someone we knew. You could never prepare yourself to be ready. But the one I never forgot was when Mama's cousin, Mehdi, and his three children got killed along with his wife's parents and her two younger sisters. They all got killed in one bomb explosion. His wife, Sara was sleeping safely at the hospital after she'd given birth to their son. A few hours prior, Mehdi had dropped his three children at his in-laws and rushed to the hospital himself to be with Sara. After she gave birth, he went back to pick the kids up. Mehdi arrived just in time for the bomb to hit Sara's house, killing Sara's parents, her sisters, her children and Mehdi. I heard Sara lost her mind when she *heard what had happened that night and had never recovered. No one could be really safe anywhere, even schools were targeted. As for me, I didn't fear for myself anymore, but I worried sick about my family and Pooya, especially for Pooya.*

Surprisingly, one afternoon I received a letter from him; Shiva brought it to me. He wrote how bad things were in the south. He wrote how soldiers, boys like him, were killed before his eyes. "We're in bad shape, we are losing the war," he wrote, and he was right.

Since America and most European countries supported Iraq at that time, the remaining countries had turned down Iran's call for help. They were too scared to help. On top of that, America's sanction was hurting Iran. Considering all that, Iraq had conquered a few villages. Khoramshahr, another big city in the south surrounded and Abadan, the heart of Iran's oil, had been partially taken. Iraq took tourist-attracted islands such as Kish and Khark. Those islands were important to Iran's economy; most of the merchants' trading used to take place there before the war.

There were thousands of refugees from the south who escaped to other parts of Iran and that alone caused much chaos and made the people more devastated. People who had lost everything in the south were seeking shelter, food, and money and, of course, it resulted in the escalation of the crime rate, pure chaos. Yes, Pooya was right; we were in bad shape and losing the war.

Grandma Fariba took a letter from her treasure box and opened it with her shaky hands. She asked me to read it aloud, Pooya wrote:

To my dearest,
Dear Fariba, I'm writing this letter to you while we're waiting for an order. We don't know what the command might be. Capitan Gerami may want us to go ahead with plan "A" which means to attack.
Or he may order to reposition, that is our plan "B".
I must tell you my love; waiting for those orders is a killer.

Fariba darling, you can't possibly know how much I want to see you and to hold you in my arms. There is a picture of you in my head and its copy is in my heart. This way you're always with me. You're with me during these cold nights in the desert.

You're with me during those long days when the hot sands burn our skin every time the wind blows.

It is you, who gives me the strength and patience.

Fariba, I feel sad. I cried the other day, for most of my friends are either wounded or dead.

The enemy is vicious and knows no God.

I can't wait for this War to be over. The sight of blood and The smell of burned flesh makes me sick to my stomach.

What are we fighting for anyway?

We don't have supplies.

There is not enough food for soldiers.

We're in bad shape, Fariba.

But some of these boys are real heroes. They're really brave and Make me real proud to be next to them.

My beautiful Fariba, we have to go, the order has arrived. It's plan "A".

I have to go now. Bye my love, my angel.

Pooya

Next to his name I saw a drawing of a little heart, and in it he wrote "FARIBA" in capital letters.

Grandma continued:

Six long, suffering months had passed since Pooya had gone to the south. In August, I stayed home most of the time due to a suffocating heat. Pooya's letters had been arriving more regularly that summer. I could not send him any myself.

"They keep moving me from location to location and I may not receive it," he wrote once before.

Sealed and protected, my letters were all addressed to Shiva. The ones that were meant for me had an "X" at the corner of the envelope, hers didn't. Shiva delivered them to me as soon as she got them. I wanted to be strong, as he wanted me to be. I tried to be positive and to have faith. I wished for the war to be over so Pooya could return; only if I knew the game of destiny or what faith had planned for me, only if I knew.

I remember that summer, four years earlier in September I had met the man of my dreams. I had planned to send him a card for our anniversary despite the fact that he told me not to send him letters. I wanted him to know how my heart yearned for him, how I loved him and prayed for his safe return. I missed him and he needed to know how I felt.

I went to the store, picked up a proper card and hurried home. At home I saw a couple of strangers in our living room.They were busy talking with Papa and didn't see me come in. I didn't think much of them. Eager to write my thoughts of passion I ran up the stairs to go to my room. Before I could reach the last step, I heard Papa calling my name.

"Fariba."

I stopped to answer him. "Yes, Papa."

Papa reached the stairs. "I thought I heard you come in. Would you please come downstairs, I would like you to meet our guests."

I don't know exactly why, but I felt a sense of wariness inside. I went down the stairs and followed Papa to the living room. Next to Mama, sitting on our big sofa, an old woman smiled and at the corner, a middle-aged man who looked too comfortable sitting on my favorite blue chair, bowed.

"Fariba I would like you to meet Mrs. Taban and her son, Mr. Mehrdad.

"It's nice to meet you." I said with a smile and panicked inwardly at the same time. Somehow I had a bad feeling about the purpose of that meeting and before long, I knew why.

"Fariba, they came to ask permission for your hand in marriage," Papa said. By his happy face, I judged he already had approved them.

I didn't realize my expression had changed until I heard Mr. Mehrdad say, "Oh…don't worry I'm not the one. Please don't be that scared; it's for my younger brother." He laughed.

"We own that big supermarket on Apadana Avenue, the one that is called Taban Market. I'm sure you've seen it," the man said.

"Yes, I've seen it. That's a very nice supermarket," I commented. I didn't know what else to say, I wanted to cry instead; my voice sounded rickety, too.

"Miss Fariba why don't you come and sit here next to me?" Mrs. Taban asked. She pointed at the sofa and grinned, revealing her big set of ugly teeth; I already hated the sight of her. Truly, she looked ugly and fat, nothing like Mama. My mother was pretty and certainly not fat. I went and sat next to her as she requested. I could smell the perfume she wore. A cheap Arabic perfume people used to bring from Saudi Arabia. I didn't like it.

"I'm sure Mr. and Mrs. Abari wouldn't mind if we ask Miss Fariba to loosen up her chadoor a little so we can see her better. My son here is like her father. You don't mind, Mr. Abari, do you? People say there is no harm in one quick look." She smiled again as she asked Papa.

I didn't like the way she talked. 'So we can see her better,' I mimicked her in my head with rage. I wasn't a 'thing' for her to look at, just to see if she likes it or not. 'Papa would never ask me to loosen up my chadoor. He'll throw them out for her rudeness,' I thought in relief as I waited for Papa to roar with anger.

"Of course, after all we are going to be family. Fariba, why don't you take your chadoor off, honey?" Papa asked. 'What?' I wondered. 'What just happened here? Did Papa ask me to remove my chadoor?' I couldn't believe it!

I felt like merchandise, being priced. Unwillingly I took off my veil. It didn't bother me a bit that my hair looked messy and not combed.

"My…you've got beautiful long hair, I must say," she said to me. "Your daughter is very beautiful." She turned to Mama. "I dreamed to find a girl like Miss Fariba for my darling son." She kept on smiling

as she talked. I glanced at her teeth again, they looked worse than I thought. Oh, how I hated her and both her sons; even my supposedly future husband, the one who hadn't come with them. 'Why aren't they leaving? How long do I have to sit here with my fake smiles?' I wanted to ask Mama, but of course I didn't.

"My son Manoochehr is a very nice man. He has always been perfect," she said. Her cheap perfume started to suffocate me.

"Oh, yes. My brother has so many qualities. He has a head for business. If it wasn't for him, our supermarket wouldn't be what it is today," Mr. Mehrdad advertised his brother. He too looked ugly, fat and old, maybe in his sixties.

"He is my younger brother, but I have to be fair. I'll give him the credit for our business," he added.

"Oh, yes. That's true you know." The woman started to talk. "My Manoochehr is very smart and I…"

I couldn't listen to them talk anymore. I felt sick. The more they talked about their beloved son and brother, the more I wanted to vomit. I couldn't take it any longer.

"Papa, may I be excused for a moment?" I asked.

"Yes, dear," he answered. However, he didn't seem so happy about my request. I saw the frown that formed on Papa's forehead as he said, "Yes, dear." But did I care? I think not, because I got up and walked upstairs to my room, closed the door and froze right behind it. I just stood there; my head leaned against the hard wooden door, my fists clenched against my chest. I wanted to bang my head onto the wall, but stood frozen as an ice pack, I remained motionless. My chest moved up and down as each breath sent the suffocating air into my lungs and then out. I thought that I would have a heart attack, but I didn't. I wish I did, if I could just die. I felt dizzy; I walked toward my bed with effort and crashed there. The whole room spanned and started to spin.

'How do I get out of this now?' I nervously asked myself. Mama came to my room about twenty minutes later as my mind continued to search for a way out.

"*Fariba, aren't you coming back downstairs?*" *she asked. I didn't answer.*

"*Our guests are still waiting for you,*" *she added.*

"*No, Mama, I have a terrible headache, I…I can't.*"

"*But Fariba they—*"

"*Please, Mama,*" *I interrupted her.* "*Please leave me be for a moment.*" *Mama looked at me in a strange way. I saw her right eyebrow lift upward.*

"*Do you want me to bring you something for the headache?*" *she managed to say calmly.*

"*No thanks, Mama, I have already taken Acetaminophen.*" *I lied of course. What headache? Although, I got one nasty headache later on as I thought about what I did.*

It seemed like a nightmare. They wanted to cage me with a marriage I didn't want, with a husband I didn't love and I responded by running to my room. What could that fix? Nothing, except making matters worse by getting my parents angry, as they perhaps tried to find a good excuse for my impolite behavior. Perhaps my parents were dying of shame for what I'd done. Leaving the guests and not returning back? Simply rude; I must have shattered their mirror image. No, no forget about them all and how they felt. It was I, who they shattered in pieces and nothing could put me back together. I cried.

The next few days nobody talked about Taban's family. Surprised and yet relieved, I wished for it to stay that way. 'Maybe Papa didn't like them after all,' I hoped. How I needed Pooya to be there for me; to hold me and tell me not to worry. I suddenly remembered I didn't even mail the postcard yet. The last few days, my mind had been occupied with Taban's family and how to get rid of them should they pop up in our living room again.

"**W**ould you please take Zina to the library today?" Mama asked me. "She needs to get a book for her school project. Please help her choose the right one."

"Yes Mama," I replied. I didn't mind getting out anyway.

At the library, after we sat at a table, Zina started to read her chosen book as I floated in the river of my own thoughts. I hadn't heard anything about the famous "T" family in the past two weeks. 'It's a good sign,' I thought happily. Surely Papa didn't like something about them or, maybe they didn't like my bad manners when I left the room and never came back downstairs. That had to be it. That ugly, fat old woman didn't like what I did. I smiled with enthusiasm.

"Why are you smiling?" Zina asked.

"Why aren't you reading?" I asked back.

"I was, until you smiled."

"So," I said. In reality, I wanted to pull her hair and say, "You annoy me."

"People don't smile for no reason!"

"Well, I do. I smile for no reason. Now read, and this time pay attention to what you read," I ordered her. She was always the nosy one.

"I know why you're smiling."

"Oh really, what am I smiling about, miss know it all?" I said with ridicule.

"You're smiling because you're going to be a bride soon."

"Bride! You silly, I'm not going to be a bride."

"Yes you are. You don't have to hide it from me."

"Who gave you that idea?"

"I heard that myself from Mama."

"What?" I almost jumped on her. "What did you hear?"

"Oops,… nothing." She started to read again.

"You better tell me right now what you have heard, or else," I ordered as I closed her book.

"Hey…what are you doing? I'll tell Mama that you didn't let me read," she protested.

"You tell her a word and see what I'll do to all your dolls. Plus, I'll tell her that you didn't do your homework the other day," I threatened and Zina became quiet.

"I'm waiting," I told her.

"Well...I..." she stopped.

"Spit it out." I ordered again quietly but harshly.

"I heard Mama when she talked on the phone with Auntie Firoozeh. She told her that Papa had already talked to Mr. Taban and your wedding is going to be next month and..."

Zina had not finished her sentence yet and the whole library started to spin around me. I pulled myself together and asked, "Are you sure? Because I'll kill you if you're making this up."

"I swear to God, Fariba. Your wedding is next month."

I couldn't think anymore; I drew a blank. I told Zina to get the book and we returned home.

Zina begged me not to tell Mama that I heard it from her and I promised that I wouldn't say anything. I felt devastated and betrayed. I knew that if Pooya had been here, he would have reconsidered my idea of running away together this time. But he wasn't here and I needed him so much. Far and away, Pooya had no clue and how could I deal with this awful situation alone? How could I get out of it?

The only way out, however hair-raising, seemed to be the sole option I had left; tell my parents I loved someone else. 'They would kill me,' I thought. Did it matter? Of course it didn't matter, not if they forced me to marry someone other than Pooya. Strangely enough, my parents had not said a word to me yet. They were acting as if I didn't have to know about my own upcoming wedding.

As I promised Zina, I didn't want to bring the subject up myself. Instead, I waited for a clue. The clue came out from Bibi's mouth the next day. She came to clean our house and to wash the curtains.

As she started to bring down the white curtains in the living room she said, "You know, Mrs. Abari, for the past few weeks we didn't have air attacks and I couldn't help thinking maybe it'll never happen again."

Bibi came down the ladder, caught a few deep breaths, and continued, "But last night's air attack took all my hopes away. I felt so scared as if my life had come to an end."

"Don't let a few weeks of calm fool you, Bibi. The war is not going to finish soon. I have a feeling that worse is yet to come," Mama said. She gave Bibi a glass of water.

"But you know, Mrs. Abari, I'm glad that with all this happening, people still celebrate and have happy moments. God knows how I enjoy weddings. I'm so happy for Miss Fariba. God willing, soon I'll do this kind of cleaning for Miss Ferry, too." The clue I waited for, just found its way to me. "What is Bibi talking about Mama?" I asked immediately.

"Bibi, you ruined it," Mama told Bibi as her right eyebrow went upward again.

"She ruined what? Mama, what did she ruin?"

"I may as well tell you now. We wanted to surprise you; lately you were kind of down," Mama said. "We set up your wedding for next month." She clapped her hands out of joy like a child. Mama's face became one big smile, but I didn't smile. How could I?

"My wedding! Who am I marrying, Mama? Who is supposed to be my future husband?" I felt pain all over as I asked that question.

"You surely remember the Tabans, don't you? Remember that nice lady who came here with one of her sons?" She paused as she saw me standing there like a statue instead of jumping for joy. "Remember, they were here about three weeks ago?" Mama wanted me to recollect.

Remember? She didn't know, not only did I recall their visit but also those thoughts never had left me. Day and night, the memory of the Tabans was like a nightmare.

"Yes, Mama, I remember her big teeth and her awful Arabic perfume."

"Fariba, what has got into you? Lately you make fun of everybody that comes here."

"Maybe I don't want to marry. Maybe I'd like to fall in love with my husband before I say, "yes". Maybe I—"

"Bite your tongue; falling in love!" Mama interrupted me rudely. "Who's teaching you all this nonsense? All about love and—"

"Maybe I'm tired of all the people who want to find me a husband." This time it was I who interrupted her. I continued as her jaw dropped. "I hate all of you; you make plans for my wedding without telling me, as if I don't count," I yelled.

"Fariba, you're beside yourself," she yelled back. I ignored her and ran toward the stairs to repeat what I loved to do most in times of crisis; run to my room to hide away.

"Don't worry, Mrs. Abari. She's shocked and nervous. All girls react that way at first." I heard Bibi say to Mama as I reached the stairs, crying. Why couldn't I just say I loved someone else? Would that make a difference? Would that make them feel for me and stop the whole thing? Or would Papa just kill me? Finally, I came to the conclusion that no matter what they did to me, no other choice remained but to tell them the truth.

The next morning, while having breakfast, Papa seemed excited. He kept talking about my upcoming wedding. I figured Mama had told him how Bibi had ruined the surprise and I knew all about it. Knowing Mama, I could swear she left the most important part out, my outrage. I sat there and listened to Papa as he went on and on about the arrangements and wedding plans.

"Why are you so quiet, Fariba? You haven't said a word the entire morning." Papa had finally noticed. I didn't answer, not a word, not even a shrug.

"Aren't you happy? You have found a rich young husband!" Mama asked and then commented. Why did she have to act as if yesterday's conversation never happened? I wondered.

"I don't know him. I don't love him; how can I be happy?"

"Fariba, darling, you're going to know him and love him, too, just like any good wife would," Mama told me as she tapped on my shoulder.

"I saw him," Papa said happily. "He's a nice guy, good looking man, too."

'What? Papa, you actually think that if you liked him, I would, too? What are you thinking?' I wanted to yell. 'What are you all thinking? Is this supposed to make me feel any better that Papa saw him? What about me? I didn't see him.' I wanted to scream. Although silently tortured, I remained quiet and swallowed a big painful knot in my throat.

Papa continued, "I asked a few friends of mine who happen to know them well. They have told me that not only are the Tabans rich, but they're also respectable and nice people. In fact…"

Papa went on about how good they were and how happy I would be as their daughter-in-law. He talked as my mind escaped to my own world until his laughter brought me back to theirs again.

"Do you know he has a big house on top of the hill in Darvazeh-Shiraz? Mr. Taban said that you're going to live----."

"Papa, would you please stop it." I interrupted him. "Please Papa. I don't care what you think about him. Can any of you hear me? I don't want him," I screamed. I saw Mama's eyes widened and a big frown formed on Papa's face. Immediately I regretted what I'd said. I couldn't stop it anymore, too late. I had to just finish what I had started. 'No more regret, no more fear,' I decided.

"I don't want to marry Mr. Taban. I don't care how rich he is or how beautiful his house would be. I love somebody else." There, I said it and it felt as if the entire world silenced and turned to stare at me. I didn't care if the world crashed down on my head at that point.

"I love someone else Papa". I said it again. "I love Pooya…I love Pooya." I cried like a child as I repeated my last sentence. Except for my own weeping sound, an awful silence overwhelmed the room. I knew that any minute would be a burst of anger from my parents, the intolerable calm before the storm and it didn't take long before the storm hit.

"Are you out of your mind? How dare you talk about loving another man? How dare you?" Papa yelled as his clinched fist came down hard on the table.

"We didn't raise you this way. I can't believe my own ears. I won't let you bring shame on our family. How dare you disrespect us by talking like this?"

He kept on yelling. I never saw Papa that furious before, but I didn't care. I wasn't going to be Taban's bride, no matter what the price. Ready to fight and pay for it, I stood my ground. Mama remained quiet and shocked by the whole event.

Papa got up and stood beside me. "You're going to marry this man like I tell you to, and that's the end of it. This wedding will take place as soon as possible; I'm going to make sure of it," he said with his finger pointed at me.

"Oh no, Papa, please...have mercy...please, Papa."

I cried aloud as I got up from my chair and kneeled before him. I held his left leg and pleaded hard. "Papa, please, I love Pooya very much. I will kill myself if you force me to marry Taban. Don't you understand Papa?"

"Oh yes, I understand that you have to be ashamed of yourself. I understand that you are going to bring disgrace to our family with your behavior."

"Papa, I haven't done anything wrong. Pooya and I love each other. There is no crime, no shame in that. We—"

"Stop," he yelled. "You make my blood boil. Enough is enough. You are to marry Taban. If you want to kill yourself, go ahead. That's better than the shameful sin you have committed."

He pushed me back in order to free his leg from my tight grip.

"God help you if I ever hear any more nonsense coming out of your mouth," he yelled again.

I remained on the floor as I wept. Mama never moved from her chair the entire time, nor spoke a word. Papa started to walk up and down the length of the dining room. He lit his cigarette, then came to the table and stood there.

"Who is that boy? I swear to God I'll kill him. What was his name again?" he asked in rage. I didn't answer. I didn't even raise my head up to look at him.

"Answer me," he ordered. I could hear the sound of his teeth squeezing out of fury.

"Who is he?" he asked me again. "How long have you known him?"

"His name is Pooya, and we have known each other for about four years. Papa we didn't do anything wrong, we just talked."

"Hush, you just answer what you're asked. Otherwise remain quiet. Do you hear?"

"Yes, Papa."

Papa sat on the chair, on the other side of the table and put his cigarette down on the ashtray. "Where does he live?" he asked.

"He lives with his family, on Mir Avenue."

"I need his complete address. I want to teach him a lesson he will never forget."

"Papa, he's fighting in the south. He's not here now."

"Lucky for him; God help him if I see him."

"But he didn't do anything, Papa. He's—"

"Stop talking...be quiet. Get out of this room before I lose control and hit you. Your mother and I have your wedding to plan," he roared like an injured lion. I had never seen Papa like that.

I left the room as he wished and secured myself in the comfort of my room, my own little sanctuary.

~

*T*he following day, Papa began his punishment by not speaking to me, as if I didn't exist, and to be honest I didn't mind it. I couldn't face him. The thought of him asking more questions about Pooya horrified me.

More and more I isolated myself in my room, trying to work my brain up to find a solution to that madness. Finally, I found a way out. As they continued planning my wedding, I began analyzing a plan of my own, a plot to escape.

Three weeks later, things were as bad as they were before. Papa still ignored me and Mama only talked when necessary. A cold, uncomfortable atmosphere polluted our house. It felt alien and strange; we never had a situation where we didn't talk to our parents and vice versa. But I couldn't let things pollute my brain, too, could I? I had to concentrate on my own plan and it did seem like a right route for me to take, a direct path to freedom. Over the years, I had saved enough money from my allowances that could buy me a ticket to go to Mashad and pay for a week stay in a small cheap motel. Untouched by war in the north of Iran, Mashad seemed to be a perfect city. Over there, I could find a job in a store or a supermarket. 'Even better, since I know how to make dresses, maybe I could find a job in a tailor's shop,' I thought with enthusiasm. I had to let Pooya know what I had planned and where I needed to go.

A week before my wedding, I received a phone call from Shiva. She sounded strange and wanted to talk to me right away. Eager to see her myself, I wanted to tell her about my decision. Shiva came to my house that afternoon. My parents still didn't know anything about Shiva's connection to the boy I loved. They thought of her as a classmate and new friend from high school. It shocked me when I saw her that day; she looked sick, pale and her eyes were puffy.

"Shiva what's wrong? Are you sick?"

"Fariba…I need to talk to you. I'm afraid…." She didn't finish her sentence.

"What? You're afraid of what?" I asked her.

"Oh, Fariba, I don't know how to start…I have bad news."

Without saying a word, I just looked at her to continue.

"There was a battle near Ahvaz where Pooya and the rest of his group were." With her voice shaking, she added, "They said that Iranian soldiers were surrounded and…"

Suddenly, she started to cry; her whole body trembled. I sat her down, sat next to her myself and held her.

"Why are you crying? Please tell me."

"Pooya is dead Fariba. He's dead. He was killed," she repeated as she howled.

"Stop it, Shiva." I pulled my arms back to myself and stood up. "I said stop it…I know what you're trying to do now."

Shiva raised her head and looked at me in a strange way, as if she didn't understand what I was saying to her. She stopped crying and the room became quiet.

Finally, she asked, "Did you hear what I just said?"

"Yes, of course I heard you and like I said I know what you're doing." I smiled. "But it's okay. Everything is under control, Shiva. I'm going to tell you what I have planned," I said with vigor. Shiva looked at me as if I had lost my mind. She seemed really confused. I kept talking, completely ignoring her dazed face.

"I know that somehow you must have heard about my upcoming wedding next week. Who told you, Bibi? I shouldn't have given you her address when you said your mother wanted to hire a maid. Bibi talks too much." As I told her that, I saw Shiva's jaw drop and her eyes widen.

"Oh...you..." I said. "You're a very good actress, Shiva, pretending you know nothing about this." Shiva didn't speak. I will never forget the look on her face. Now, when I think about that moment I can visualize everything. Poor her, she looked baffled as she sat motionless without saying a word and listened as I talked.

"So, now that you've heard I'm getting married, you want to punish me for not waiting for Pooya. You're just trying to scare me, right?" I smiled again.

She didn't answer, didn't smile either. At that time, I couldn't say what went on in her head. She just seemed to be speechless and couldn't move a muscle.

I went to my window and looked far into the distance at the Sofeh Mountain and explained, "Well, what you heard is true. My wedding is supposed to be next week. But you see, I'm going to run away; I won't be here." I turned my head away from the window and looked right into her bewildered eyes.

"I will go somewhere far away and wait there until Pooya comes back." I continued to explain, "I have thought of everything and all is ready. I will leave tomorrow before sunset. I will—"

"Fariba, I don't know what you're talking about," she interrupted me. Shiva got up, came toward me and grabbed both my shoulders.

I must tell you she walked fast for a person whose muscles weren't moving earlier.

"I'm not trying to scare you. I didn't know anything about your wedding…Fariba, what I said is true. Pooya is dead. Don't you understand? He got killed."

Tears rushed out from the corners of her eyes and ran down her cheeks as she said those words. I froze. I couldn't blink or move for a few seconds. This time it was I who couldn't move a muscle. I didn't say a word. Instead, I stared at her. I gazed at her tears, at her face. Only then did a blast of reality hit me. I pushed her hands off of my shoulders and went a few steps away from her.

"No, God, no. It isn't true." My chin trembled and I couldn't speak; I started to cry.

"Oh, Fariba. I'm very sorry…I feel the same; I feel awful," Shiva said as she came closer.

"No. This isn't true…it isn't true, it just can't be. It's not true…. They always make mistakes, you know." I talked and cried and then for a moment, hope sparkled in my aching heart. "Maybe he was taken as a prisoner of war."

"I wish that was the case. But somebody identified him…. There is no mistake. They said…"

She kept on talking, but I couldn't hear anything anymore. I started to cry louder and became hysterical to the point where I couldn't even breathe. How should I describe that moment? I felt extreme anger, combined with sorrow. Angry at the world, angry with people, I felt angry at everything and everybody. Fate had crushed and destroyed my whole existence. My world turned into this vast empty dark space; a pure nightmare that I couldn't wake up from.

Pooya meant everything to me and with him gone, I had lost everything. My life didn't matter anymore.

That night after Shiva left, I made my decision. I had to join Pooya; I wanted to. My plan had changed. I didn't need to run away anymore. Where I wanted to go didn't need much planning. It was easy, almost too easy. I wanted to do it as soon as possible. I had to.

'No point for me to live another day,' I thought. Therefore, I decided to kill myself that very night. I took out Pooya's letters and started to read them all over again one by one. I kissed them so many times; for I knew his hands wrote those words and his fingers had touched the papers. I cried over and over especially when I read this poem, the one he copied from a book, his favorite:

I know for each drop of tear that falls on the ground,
A flower would grow and a butterfly would fly.

And then, he wrote:

I know that I would be in your heart and You would live forever in mine, and then we would never be alone.

Grandma started to cry. Her tears rushed down again just like the last time she gave me that poem to read. Her fragile body trembled under her veil. I tried to calm her down, but she didn't pay attention to me. She kept on saying something slowly, I tried to listen. "I cried and cried that night, and for each tear that fell on the ground, no flower grew and no butterfly flew," she said softly. My heart ached for her.

"Grandma I think it's enough for today, you should rest a little?" I said with concern.

"No darling, I would like to continue, unless you're tired yourself. Are you?" I told her I wasn't and then she continued:

Later that night, I waited for an hour after everybody went to their rooms to sleep. I put on a white dress and combed my hair. I even put on pink lipstick and penciled my eyes in black. In my inner world, I thought of myself as a young bride who was on her way to see the man she loved, to be his wife for all eternity. In another world, away from the land of living, Pooya and I were going to be happy.

Carefully I tiptoed to the bathroom and filled the tub with warm water. I sat in the tub and said my prayers for my family and then took a razor and slashed both my wrists. I watched the flow of blood. Fast and silent it colored the water. Its warmth felt strangely nice on my skin. I kept on bleeding, the water in the tub turned red. I continued to watch myself bleed and it didn't scare me, nor at any point did I feel any regret. I knew that just like Pooya said, we would never be alone again.

It didn't take long before I felt dizzy and extremely weak. I watched my own image in the long, large mirror on the wall across from the bathtub, I smiled. I knew that I would join Pooya soon. After a while, I reached a point when I couldn't keep my eyes open anymore and became very cold. I started to shiver. Certainly not a good feeling, but I didn't mind it at all. One last time, I looked at my face in the mirror; it had no color except for my lips, they looked bluish. All of a sudden, the bathroom seemed brighter and even colder than before; I could feel the chill all over my body. I closed my eyes and then everything became dark. I felt weightless, as if somebody had lifted me and I floated in space. After that, I didn't feel anything anymore.

~

I opened my eyes in a white surrounding. I didn't know where I was; it looked like a room, but I couldn't say for sure. Everything looked fuzzy, and very unclear. Quickly I floated back in space. I don't know how long I remained in that weightless state, floating. But I remember how the room looked very clearly the next time when I opened my eyes again.

Lying in a bed in a hospital room, my wrists were both covered with bandages. A bag full of blood hung from a pole and a tube delivered the substance of life into my veins. Slowly I turned my head to my left. I saw Mama, sitting next to my bed, her puffy, red eyes fixed on me. She bent toward me and said something. I couldn't hear her well; then again she spoke with a low voice.

"Why, Fariba...why?" she cried and this time I heard her. I didn't feel strong enough to talk, nor did I want to explain why. So, I remained quiet and I turned my head away from her sad face. She leaned back onto her chair and halted; I felt bad for her. At the same time I felt angry, why didn't I die?

Later, I found out how and why I didn't die as Mama explained everything. An air attack took place that night and my family rushed to the basement as we always did during those attacks. When Papa realized I wasn't there with them, he ran upstairs to search for me and that's how he found me. He rushed me to the nearest hospital where they were able to successfully pour a life I didn't want back into my every cell. Ironic, isn't it? An attack took Pooya's life, while another saved mine.

~

*T*he wedding had to be postponed of course. I never told my parents why I tried to kill myself. I never said a word about Pooya's death. I assume they took my suicide attempt as an objection to the wedding. After that day, for three months I was on twenty-four hour watch. I couldn't even breathe without someone counting how many times. But all that didn't matter. Although physically not buried yet, I considered myself dead. I knew the time would come when my body would die, too; but until then, I had to carry on among the living. So I learned how to subsist. After that, I breathed in and breathed out without any purpose. I walked, but I didn't have any destination in mind. I made others happy by doing what they wanted me to do. I became a clown; laughing on the surface and yet inwardly, crying. I lived without a soul, a picture perfect living dead.

As for the Taban family, they were never told the real reason behind the delay. They didn't know that I tried to commit suicide. "Fariba became sick and needed to be hospitalized," my father had told them. That's exactly how he said it, not a word less, nor did he explain more. Mrs. Taban came and visited me in the hospital and then at home, too. In those visits I never saw my husband to be "Manoochehr". I didn't care to see him anyway; I wanted for them and everybody else to leave me alone and let me be or even better, let me die. That's all I wanted. But I never had the luxury of having what I fancied those days and nothing could make the Taban family disappear. They waited only enough time for me to get back on my *feet and back to my hollow life before they completed the last wedding preparations. So, despite all that had happened, arrangements were made without any further delay. The two families were moving full speed toward the matrimonial event.*

Everybody seemed too busy to notice the gloom in my eyes. I assume my lifeless face and my silence didn't bother anyone. Did my parents ever stop to think how I felt? I wondered sometimes, but I didn't think they cared to know. They had become so alienated. I felt as if I didn't know them anymore. They had decided who I had to marry, when and where it had to take place and I had no right to make any decision about my own future.

Chapter 4

*F*inally *in March, just when spring began, I married Manoochehr
and became Mrs. Taban. I can never forget that awful day. The
horror began early that day when my mother-in-law took us to a
salon of her choice to get our grooming done. Lady Saha, a beautician
she had known for years came to greet us with a big smile. Her fiery
red, long hair made her skin seem too pale. She appeared to be in
her fifties, tall and slender; I should say, for a woman of her age, she
looked fit.*

'Pretty, if one can see beyond the heavy make-up,' I thought.

*"Lady Saha must have been a very pretty woman in her youth,"
I whispered in Ferry's left ear to share my thought. Ferry nodded in
agreement.*

*The woman started her work and kept us company by telling so
many stories. She gossiped and I have to admit she did it well. She
had a unique way of telling tales that kept everyone focused on the
stories. No one fussed over their hair and make-up and not a single
person seemed to realize how slow she worked.*

*'What a smooth talker and a gossiper,' I thought again later, but
this time I kept it to myself and didn't share it with Ferry. I looked*

at everyone and everything and I thought how happy they all seemed to be. Everybody looked animated. I sat on a red chair, observing the parlor. Mostly in red with touches of white here and there, the salon looked bizarre. I never had seen a room that red in my entire life. Personally, I didn't like her taste and I definitely felt unease at being one of her coloring books. The woman had no clue about color harmony, I could see that clearly when I looked deep into her made up face, done in all the wrong shades.

Finally, Lady Saha asked me to put my wedding gown on and then she covered it with a long plastic cape and started to work on me. She turned my chair away from the mirror and every time I tried to see myself she didn't let me. "Wait until I'm done, my dear," she said. "Boy, this bride is so eager to see herself in the mirror," she said to everybody and everyone laughed and Mama bit her lip in shame as she looked at me with her eyebrow lifted upward.

When she finished with my hair and make-up, she asked me to get up. As I stood, she took the long protective cape off and turned me toward the large mirror. I took a look at myself as a bride for the first time. I looked like a porcelain doll with a white face and a red circle on each of my cheeks. My lipstick looked awfully red; my eyelashes were twice as long and heavy with layers of thick black mascara. In the mirror I looked into the eyes of a different person with a face so alien, so unfamiliar. Teased up in a twist and bejeweled with lots of little white pearls, my hair seemed surprisingly perfect.

I stood there staring at myself. My exquisite wedding gown, elegantly tailored with lots of pearl work still lacked the power to pour life into my dead heart. I confess, the gown could make a happy bride glow beautifully, but its splendor worked no magic for a bride whose heart was filled with despair. I took a deep look at myself again. The man I wanted to marry was dead. Did I really care how I looked as a bride? Clearly, it didn't matter. I turned around to find Mama.

Still sitting on a chair at the far corner to my left, she looked all ready. She had the happy satisfied face of any proud mother who saw her first born as a bride for the first time. She looked nice in general, I have to say, except her skin looked weird under the heavy make-

up and thick foundation; her skin looked more like a statue than anything else. Ferry and Zina's hair styles, although nice, seemed wrong for their age. Thank God they didn't have to wear make-up. Only married women were allowed to paint their faces. Mrs. Taban had a big smile and, for some reason, she reminded me of the ugly witch in Zina's story book.

When lady Saha finished turning everybody into living statues we returned to my parents' house for the wedding ceremony. A formal procedure to put an end in to the life I knew, to bury me into a life I didn't want and didn't care about. My heart wept as I entered our house. I felt so much sorrow as I looked around. Lots of people were there already. I would only see my so called husband, Manoochehr, after we were married. He and all the other men were downstairs.

Our house looked different, too; someone had turned it into a huge wedding hall. Wooden tables and chairs replaced our house furniture. Huge flower arrangements garlanded each corner as miniature roses in crystal vases adorned every table. The room looked a lot bigger. All the female guests and I remained upstairs. I knew after the ceremony when the marriage certificate was signed, Manoochehr would come upstairs to join me, and then I would see him for the first time.

I know it's strange and hard to digest for someone like you to understand the notion of such a wedding when the bride and groom had never met before, but it used to happen back then and it may still happen in some families. Grandma explained and then continued:

That wasn't my family's idea, but the Tabans were extremely old fashioned and they came up with all the rules. Not all weddings were like that, keeping men and women separated. Complete gender segregation only happened in very religious families like the Tabans and of course no one could object when things were wrapped in the name of religion and marked by religious beliefs.

When my husband finally came to the room and sat next to me, I didn't want to look at him. Believe it or not, to me, it didn't matter how he looked. I didn't even want to be there. If it wasn't for Mama who poked me in the arm and ordered me to face him, I would have just continued to ignore that stranger sitting next to me. She poked me twice, before I turned left toward Manoochehr. 'Would these people be able to see the hatred I'm feeling and know why I'm so reluctant to look at Manoochehr?' I wondered and hoped they wouldn't.

"She's so cute, look how bashful she is," one unfamiliar voice said in the crowd.

"Don't be shy now; he's your husband," I heard someone else say. If only they knew, how I felt. If they only knew how hard I tried not to grab the silver knife to stab him in the chest. 'God I want to vomit,' I thought with fear.

Forcefully, I turned to him, hoping that the white sheer veil would hide my hatred. He pulled the veil up. My cold stare showed no emotion as he looked at me. Did he ever realize how empty I felt? Did he ever know my heart held nothing except hate? Did he notice the blank lifeless look in my face? I always wondered.

His bald head, round face and dark eyes didn't look anything like my father had described before. His thick mustache could hardly cover up his ugly smile with yellow teeth. His breath smelled like cigarettes. Short and chubby, by far he looked anything but handsome.

He, too, had never seen me before. He only pictured me through the descriptions given by his family. I guess he trusted their judgment. I don't remember for how long he kept on looking at me. Sickened by his stare, I wanted the ceremony to be over. Alas, every minute passed like eternity. Finally, we exchanged rings. Mine had a big diamond on top and I didn't like it. Almost all the women standing around bent over to look at my ring. 'Yes, look, look at my big wedding ring. Look, so you can go and gossip about it,' I wanted to yell at everybody. 'Look how it shines. Would you ever believe it if I told you its shimmer bothers my eyes and injures my heart?' my heart yelled out. Of course, nobody heard.

After exchanging rings, I couldn't remember what had to be done next. I had seen so many weddings and yet my brain drew a blank. Still clueless, I saw him dipping the tip of his small finger into a glass of honey and then lifted his hand up to my lips for me to suck the honey off his finger. 'Oh, that,' I remembered. Now I had to do the same for him. By doing so, the couple promises to make each other's life as sweet as honey. "Sweet", what a word that was and how strange it felt. A poison would have been far sweeter to me than that honey.

After that, all guests gathered around to present their gifts. Lots of people offered jewelry and I had to wear it immediately. Some handed envelopes with money, which Manoochehr kept. At the end, with all the jewelry that hung down my neck and covered my wrists, I still looked like a porcelain doll, but a shimmering one.

Everything about that night bothered me: the flashes of the cameras, the noises and the kisses. Piercing laughers, loud conversations, all seemed to be an echo of meaningless words and sounds.

Let me tell you, on my wedding day I felt more like a widow than a bride. A widow, only no one gave me a chance to grief, to mourn. My battered and lamented heart was veiled perfectly behind the flawless white bridal gown. Spotless as those pearls, I looked perfect. No one suspected anything to be wrong with me. No one could read me; I guess I played my role as the clown without error.

After the wedding, we drove in his white, bejeweled by red roses, Mercedes, to his big house over the hill on Darvazeh-Shiraz. One of the best neighborhoods in town, as everyone called it. Most people who were at the ceremony in my parent's house followed us to my new residence. The celebration continued until early morning hours and then the guests started to leave. I felt so tired. I just wanted everybody to leave so I could take that heavy wedding gown, and the ridiculous jewelry off. I would have given anything to just surrender my tired body to the large bed and sleep my life away. Just when I thought I could go to bed, my bedroom's door opened and Manoochehr, my husband, came inside the room. I wanted to ask him what he wanted. But when he shut the door behind him, I realized that room belonged to him, too.

He took his clothes off and went under the covers in bed. He kept looking at me with the same ugly smile that I wanted to wipe off his face so badly.

"Don't you want to sleep?" he asked me.

"Yes. I'm very tired," I answered. I can't tell you how uncomfortable I felt about the whole idea of sharing a bed with a complete stranger. I had no choice but to join him; I went and sat next to him. It felt so awkward. He started to kiss me. I felt nauseated. His hands made me feel sick to my stomach as they explored every inch of my body. Who was this man? I searched for an answer and couldn't find one; I couldn't relate to him. "Husband,…. husband". My sanity pointed that word out to bond me with him. It didn't connect me to him any more than it could connect me to the God whose existence I questioned since Pooya died.

That night, I lost my virginity to someone I didn't even know; someone I didn't love. That night, he raped me. One may say how I could call it rape if that man was no other than my own husband who took me on our wedding night. I can argue the point until the end of time, but I won't. Every single person is entitled to his or her opinion. How I looked at it, I can't call it anything but rape; only I couldn't run, nor scream for help. No one could help me.

The next morning I woke up with an annoying headache. However, I was relieved to find myself alone in the room. I didn't know when he left or where he went, nor did I want to find out. The memory of the sinister night vividly remained in my head. I curled up under the comforter, feeling cold. I wanted to lock myself in that room until the end of time. I wanted to become invisible. With my head under the covers, I listened to the silence of the room. Then I realized I couldn't erase what had happened by hiding there. I decided to get out of my imaginary shelter and keep myself busy instead. I had to find a way to stop the flashbacks of the past twenty four hours of my life. I pulled the comforter off my face and started to analyze the room. Just to take my mind off of things I studied the room profoundly.

Painted in pink, the bedroom's walls looked naked without portraits and art work. The blue comforter and yellow sheets, although made of silk, lacked style. No plants of any kind adorned the place. A breeze from an open window sneaked in to dance with the curtains; I watched as the invisible hands of the wind gently lifted the long pink lace to the air with an exotic twist. I observed the room for a while, but despite my efforts, uninvited thoughts sneaked inside my head effortlessly; I surrendered unwillingly.

I remained in bed, thinking. The reflection of the horrific wedding haunted me and I thought about how the night started and how it ended when slumber took me away. How happy I felt when I opened my eyes and didn't find that man lying next to me. 'He must have left for work,' I thought with relief.

*I lingered in bed for a long time before I decided to leave the room and get familiar with the house. Spending my time wandering around, I found a large attic right above our bedroom. My parents' house didn't have an attic, but it had a large basement; this house, on the other hand, had both. Persian rugs covered the floors wall to wall. Unlike my parents' gray based carpets, these rugs had lots of red in them. The furniture looked antique and expensive, but I found it to be in bad taste. The furniture made me feel especially sad; old people furnished their houses like that. I believed whoever singled out those settings knew nothing about colors, style or cheeriness. In my opinion, the living-room looked like an expensive furniture store where nothing matched. A large chandelier hung from the high ceiling down in the middle of a spacious salon and a matching smaller version of it dangled down in the living room. The paintings in the salon were all big, although their scenery didn't invite my eyes for a closer peek, except for one in the hall; a drawing of an old man holding a lantern walking in the dark desert got my attention. I studied that painting with fascination. Somehow it drew me inside its world. At the bottom of it I saw a name that read: **"SOHRAB"**. I remember standing there, looking at it for a while before I pulled myself away from it and walked away.*

I didn't care much for the rectangular shape of the house, but I hated its interior décor. Although, I must say, I loved its high ceilings and the garden of flowers in the backyard. I also liked the large kitchen and its chestnut wood cabinets; it reminded me of the kitchen at my parents'. The spacious shower room looked nice, especially with its ocean blue ceramic covered walls. All five oversized bedrooms faced the garden. *The living room and the "L" shaped salon both faced the porch and a big pool.*

I continued to wonder around the house until I felt hungry and decided to go find something to eat. As I entered the kitchen, I saw a middle aged woman in a shabby gray dress, preparing a fruit salad. She welcomed me with warmth and introduced herself as 'Soltan' and then asked if I wanted food and hot tea. Puzzled, I nodded and sat at the table. As she started to fix me a plate of beef kabob over rice, I realized I had heard about her before. Mom Taban had mentioned her name once, but I guessed I had forgotten it. She worked as a maid and had lived with that family for the past five years, according to what mom Taban had told me.

"I came from a nearby village, " Soltan explained while I ate. "As a widow, I have to support myself and have been doing it for years." She spoke with calm and I noticed an inner peace within her voice. I never asked about her age, but she seemed to be in her fifties.

As the days passed by, I learned to know Soltan better. Unable to find support those days, her presence offered what I yearned for. She didn't talk much, but her eyes mirrored her larger than life heart. Calm and collected, she did her chores. Most times, she tried her best to respect my privacy by giving me space to myself. Somehow she knew I needed lots of time to think and to adjust. Who knows, maybe she recognized the grief that had rooted deep inside my heart. Perhaps she saw my tears and knew how it felt to be heartbroken. After all, Soltan and I had both experienced losses. Probably she loved her husband as much as I loved my Pooya. God only knew how much I missed Pooya and how I mourned him and how I longed for him. Pooya's memories remained vivid in my head. I had nothing left of him except for the letters he wrote and how desperately I needed to hold those papers next to my heart knowing his hands had touched them, wrote them, and delivered them. I wanted to read every sentence of them, every word, all over again.

Alas, I couldn't bring them with me. I knew I couldn't keep the letters with me in my new home. So, a day before my wedding I managed to secure them in Melli Bank's safe box. I had rented a safe deposit box a year before, as Pooya had suggested back then. "You never know when you may need one," he had told me. "It's always good to have a safe place for important documents," he said. I rented one just to please him, not because I believed that I would ever have to hide things away to keep them safe. Personally, I couldn't see why; not until that day when I took the letters to the safe box. The bank had set up an automatic withdrawal from my saving account to cover the yearly fee. When I got married, I felt relieved knowing no one could find out about the letters, no one—my husband especially.

⁓

*U*nlike Soltan, Manoochehr remained a complete stranger. He had my body, but never my heart; not that he cared to possess it, nor did it matter to me. To Manoochehr, having a wife meant having someone who could take care of his needs and bear his children, so his generation would go on. He used the word "wife" as a nice wrap for the word "slave." He could never look at a woman as a soul mate, nor did he acknowledge her rights as a human being. He never really looked deep into my eyes. Sometimes I wondered if he knew what color my eyes were. Despite all that, I remained a dutiful wife, providing a fake love; a role I played painfully every day of that marriage.

Manoochehr spent his days in the Market along with his brother, from seven in the morning until late at night. His absence offered me solitude and with that I remained emotionally intact. By myself I felt peace, whether I stayed in my room, wandered around the house or went for a walk in the park. Being alone gave me a chance to be myself without having to mask my aching heart. Alone, I could mourn Pooya's death as well as my own. In the silence, I could feel Pooya's presence. He lived in my heart and existed in my dreams. Pooya's imaginary presence seemed so real; sometimes I caught myself having a loud conversation with him. What can I say? It soothed my broken heart. Those imaginary conversations helped me connect to something extraordinary. It tied me to a world different from mine.

I enjoyed every minute of the time I spent alone. Alas, my moments of solitude didn't last long when all of a sudden Manoochehr's mother decided to move out of Mehrdad's house and in with us. Having never been married, Mehrdad, her eldest son, lived in a big house all on his own and had taken his mother in after their dad passed away. I couldn't understand why on earth she wanted to come and live with us. Mehrdad had given her total authority to make the rules as the sole lady of his house. Why she wanted to leave that behind was beyond my comprehension and surely it didn't matter whether or not I understood it. Decisions were made and I got informed about it a day before she moved in.

Certainly, life under her rules wasn't easy and only became harder and harder, and time-to-time seemed impossible. She interposed and of course her highly regarded opinion reflected on almost everything we did or wanted to do. Manoochehr consulted her on every matter, even on the most ludicrous things, as if he didn't have a brain of his own. Soon, it became obvious to me that what mom Taban said, went. She turned into the puppet master and us, into puppets. My everyday life became nothing but a prewritten scenario by her. She even chose the colors of my outfits as well as everything else I needed. My opinions never mattered. I had to live her lifestyle, her thoughts and her dreams. The little sense of identity I had left in me started to vanish.

I thought with time I would get use to my new life, but I never did. I wanted to die and be buried physically, just as I had been emotionally.

My family and I visited each other from time to time. I never told them what went on or how I felt as a wife; no point to complain, anyway. Therefore, they assumed that I lived a happy and comfortable life.

As for Shiva, every time I visited my parents, I called her and we talked on the phone. I used to talk to her about everything except my marriage. I don't remember ever telling her how empty and incomplete I felt back then, but I sensed that she knew, although she never asked about my personal affairs. She never visited me in

Manoochehr's house. *"Emotionally, it is difficult for me to visit you there,"* she had told me once. *Personally, I didn't blame her for feeling that way. I didn't even ask her why she felt that way. I didn't need to ask; I knew why. Nine months after my wedding, Shiva married an engineer and a year later they left Iran for England. I felt happy for her because she sounded very content and ecstatic. I wished her an abundant life as we said a tearful goodbye.*

I could see that my life didn't have any meaning and it seemed to be more of a punishment than anything else. Destiny had sentenced me to live that life, only to be freed by the welcomed caress of the death. However, believe it or not, I learned to deal with a pointless existence for the most part. As time passed, I did everything that a wife could and would do for her husband. I remained a dutiful wife and an obedient daughter-in-law. I did spend my days making them happy while my heart mourned the death of my own identity. Truly, I did respect their authority and never asked for much myself. If it wasn't for one thing that I did secretly, I could have won the best bride/slave of the year prize. Believe me, I wouldn't have done it if I didn't think I had to; I took birth control pills without his knowledge. Emotionally, I didn't feel strong enough to be a mother; so I did what I thought was best. A couple of times, mom Taban brought up the pregnancy issue and questioned me about it. She wanted to know why I wasn't pregnant yet.

"Fariba, are you doing something to prevent pregnancy?" In the living room, my mother-in-law asked while sewing her new veil.

"No. What an odd question!" I said calmly.

"Well, more than a year has passed and you should have been pregnant by now."

She put the material away and looked at me, straight in the eye.

"Well, mom Taban, maybe you should just wait. I'm sure it will happen soon."

"Manoochehr and I have already talked about this issue. We're not so happy about it."

"What exactly are you suggesting here?" I asked.

"What I suggest is that, you better bring me a grandson and make my Manoochehr a father soon."

"And if I don't? I don't even know why you're discussing this. If there is anything to discuss, it should be between my husband and I, not him and you."

"What did you just say?" Her small eyes opened wide. "How dare you talk to me that way?" she said with anger.

I didn't answer her. She got up and as she walked out of the living room I heard her say, "I will talk to my son about your behavior." I just shrugged, ignoring her.

Manoochehr came home around eight o'clock as he usually did ever since his mother moved in with us. At the table, Mom Taban seemed to be exceptionally quiet. I knew that she was rummaging around a good opportunity to tell Manoochehr about my ill manners. Finally, her being unusually quiet did the trick and Manoochehr asked his mom what was the matter.

"I think it's better if I move out. I don't think I'm needed here."

"Why do you say that? Of course you're needed."

"Well I have to have more respect around here. You know my Mehrdad has no wife and he needs my help, but I said to myself, 'Fariba is young and inexperienced, she needs me more' and I left my poor Mehrdad alone. But what do I get in return? All I get is disrespect." Her eyes rolled and she made an innocent face as she finished talking.

"Who is disrespecting you, mother?"

"Why don't you ask your dear wife?" Manoochehr looked at me strangely. "What's going on, Fariba?"

"I don't know what she's talking about."

"Oh, you don't know, ha?" Mom Taban said as she turned toward me. "Who was the one that stood in the middle of the living room and said, 'Mom Taban, you have no right here...' Ha? Who told me that today?"

"You told my mother she has no right?" Manoochehr's eyes became rounder and bigger.

"I didn't say it that way. She asked about things that should only be discussed between you and I," I defended myself.

"Nothing is between us that she can't ask about, do you understand? She is my mother. She left her son to come here and help you. This is how you reward her?"

'Why do I have to reward her for interfering in my personal life?' I didn't dare say that, of course, I remained quiet instead. I thought it would be better to stay quiet; wrong decision.

Despite my surrender, Manoochehr became all stormy and gave me a warning, "As long as you are my wife and live here, you are to obey and respect my mother and me, do you understand?"

"Yes," I answered him.

"And I should let you know that my mom has a right to everything. You, on the other hand, should just be a devoted wife to me and a respectful daughter-in-law to my mom. Is that clear?"

"Yes," I answered again.

His ice-cold eyes brought shivers all over me as his words poured warmth into his mother's heart and she looked at me with a winner's smile on her face. I didn't say a word to him after that and neither did he say a word to me. He only talked to his mother and ignored me for the rest of the night, not that I minded. I just wanted him off my back at that moment. In fact I wanted both of them off my back. So I remained quiet and just listened to the mother and son conversation until it became late and I went to sleep. I tried my best to stay out of their way, especially hers. Only if she could stay out of mine, maybe things would have been fine. But no, she had to dig and put her nose into everything that wasn't her business.

A month later, one afternoon when I returned from a supermarket I saw her waiting for me in our kitchen. The minute I walked in, I felt something was wrong by the way she looked at me with her devilish eyes.

"Hello mom Taban…Hello Soltan," I said.

Only Soltan answered my hello. Mom Taban didn't; instead, she asked me the most awkward question.

"You haven't been a dutiful wife to my son, have you, Fariba?"

"*What on earth are you talking about?*"

"*What have you been doing? Why aren't you pregnant yet?*" she asked with anger.

"*Nothing, why do you think I'm doing something? Didn't we have this conversation just a few weeks ago? I already have told you that I'm not doing anything?*"

Mom Taban got up and walked toward me. "*You have been taking pills.*" She threw the box of birth control pills on the table right in front of me. Up to that point, I thought I had done a good job at keeping that a secret, wrong again.

"*Where...where did you get those?*" I asked her while I tried not to show any fear.

"*Where did I get these? From your jacket's pocket, that's where I got these.*" She talked loud and she looked even more furious than before.

"*You had no right to search my pockets, Mom Taban!*" It took a lot of courage for me to say that. I knew talking to her that way would get me into even bigger trouble.

"*You're telling me I have no right? Did you forget what my son said a few weeks ago? I can do anything I want; this is my son's house. I run this household.*"

"*This is my house, too, as much as it's your son's.*"

I knew that I was gambling. She came one step closer and slapped me hard. I hated her; I hated everything about her.

"*This is for answering me back, little girl. Your mother didn't do a good job bringing you up I see,*" she said. "*But wait until Manoochehr comes home and hears about your sneaky piece of work behind his back.*"

To be honest, I didn't care so much about what they would do to me: Soltan on the other hand, she looked puzzled and despite her silence, I saw fear all over her face. Still in the kitchen, listening to Mom Taban's mouth run, Manoochehr walked in. His mother didn't even wait for a second; she ran to him and showed him the pills. She told him about our conversation word for word.

Next thing, I saw his face became red with fury. He walked toward me with giant, fast steps. I went one step backward before the wall stopped me from backing away any further. I stood there helpless as Manoochehr's arm took a big swing and his hand landed strongly on my cheek. The force of his arm threw me on the floor on my left side. He started to kick me all over. He yelled and yelled and told me that he would never forgive me. That I had betrayed him and I had no right whatsoever to make any decision to take pills without his consent and knowledge.

His mother stood there and watched while I remained under his feet, being kicked and physically tortured. Soltan tried to bargain with him and asked for my forgiveness, but Manoochehr ordered her not to engage herself in family matters. Poor Soltan, she didn't know what to do. She stopped begging and just sat in the middle of the kitchen and watched the show.

I remember how I wanted to scream and beg him to stop kicking me, but I remained silent. I didn't want him to hear me say stop, I didn't want to give him the satisfaction. My arms shielded my head and face while my body took all the beatings. I wanted to die that minute, but I wouldn't let him know. I remember very well what I thought. I thought, 'Is this me under his legs? Is this me?' I had never known violence like this in my life. Papa had never done that to Mama; no, I couldn't recall seeing anything like this. Finally, he got tired of beating me and left the kitchen. I heard his mom saying something; I didn't quite get what she said and then she laughed. With my tearful eyes shut, I remained on the floor, fetus-positioned. Cold and painful, my whole body started to shake.

"Where did Manoochehr go?" Mom Taban asked Soltan and when Soltan shrugged, she said, "I better go see where he went. Manoochehr...Manoochehr..." Mom Taban called as she left the kitchen.

As soon as Mom Taban was out of sight, Soltan ran toward me and tried to help me up, but Manoochehr came back quickly and yelled at her, told her she better go to her room or else. Soltan obeyed and left the kitchen. I remained on the floor for about ten minutes or so before I could pick my battered self up.

With an effort, I went inside my room and looked at myself. I couldn't believe how terrible I looked. I had a bruised puffy circle around my left eye and a cut at the corner of my upper lip. With my arms shielding my head at all times, I couldn't remember how I got those injuries to my face. Had he kicked me in my face, too? And how was it that I couldn't remember? My legs and my back were also all bruised up; those, I expected. I looked a mess. I cleaned the cut on my upper lip with alcohol, which burned like hell and then very slowly surrendered my sore body to the soft mattress of the bed.

Since Manoochehr left the kitchen earlier that night, I didn't know where he went or what he did and to be honest I didn't care to know. But it was later around three or four o'clock in the morning that he came back to our room. Pretending to be sleep, I didn't move at all. I hoped he would just turn on his side and sleep, but I couldn't be more wrong. Violently and with a rush he pulled me in the middle of the bed and took me. I felt his rage and anger and I surrendered. Fixed on the ceiling, my eyes didn't even blink while I waited for him to satisfy himself and when he did, he simply turned his back to me and slept.

I spent the night with my eyes wide open, I couldn't sleep. Not because he made love to me that way; apart from being extra violent, the rest was just what we always did. I never participated in the lovemaking except for being there, and he never cared. I felt restless because I really didn't want to bring a child to a world like mine and without my pills, I couldn't avoid getting pregnant anymore.

The next few days, I stayed mostly in the bedroom. Soltan brought food and took care of me like a mother would. She kept putting warm and cold compresses on my injured and bruised body until I felt better. During those times when Soltan took care of me, she never asked me any question and never judged me. I heard her sigh some time to time and for so many years I wondered why she cared so much about me.

After that night Manoochehr or his mother supervised my every trip outside. Every move and conversation I made with anyone had to be watched by either one of those two. I felt like a prisoner inside a penitentiary: fenced in, with a little less air to breathe each day, trapped in a big cage called "life."

It didn't surprise me that I became pregnant soon after, I knew that would happen sooner or later. What surprised me was the fact that somehow having a baby didn't seem so bad after all. Indeed, with the baby's first kick I felt joy. Isn't it amazing how nature works sometimes?

∼

*D*uring my fifth month of pregnancy, in October, the air attacks increased. Our city Esfahan remained one of the main target sites for Iraq's warheads. The bombs were dropped by Iraqi Migs and missiles flew over our otherwise blue sky. People watched with pure horror while the missiles flew like giant snakes over our city, landing in public places, killing more innocent civilians than ever before.

People started to leave town. My parents also escaped to the north. Not far from the Russian border, they settled in a small city called Chaloos. Less affected by war, the north of Iran remained safer due to its distance from the south. Despite my parents' request and their fruitless efforts to take me with them, I had no choice but to stay. Mom Taban decided and Manoochehr agreed that it wasn't safe for me to travel in my condition. So we remained in Isfahan and had no other choice but to flee to a small village a month later. Although in the same geographic zone, the village stood far from the city. It wasn't a known place and it didn't have a large population. The small town had nothing remarkable about it to be a target; therefore, it felt safer to be there than to remain in a big city such as Esfahan. Manoocher, Mom Taban, Soltan and I settled in a very large room we rented in the back of a garden and shared the place with his brother. For me, sharing one single room with all those people I called "enemy" was hard enough, but the lack of electricity and hot water made the living conditions even harder.

In the middle of December, the bitter cold had no delay in arriving. Those times I did my best to help Soltan with the dishes whenever I could. I had to, how could I not? She wasn't young and she couldn't handle the extremely cold conditions. We washed those dishes outside the room and for that reason, such a simple task became one of the most difficult chores. Icy cold water stung like bees as it ran all over my hands. The wind blew the cold air shamelessly; it brushed against my skin like thousands of needles. Our limited gas supply didn't allow us to warm the water for every use. At times my hands were numb, swollen and red. I had cold burn patches on my face. No one else offered to help. Soltan and I cooked and cleaned and served them as if they were our guests.

I absolutely hated the fact that we had to use a public bath to take showers. I never liked those public baths. Those were large rooms with open showers all around. I wasn't used to that and I wanted to shower in a private setting, just like we had in our house. The women of the village seemed so comfortable taking baths that way. They walked around naked while having normal conversations as if they were fully dressed. While waiting for my turn, I sat there quietly as I listened to their gossip.

I felt lots of anger for the fact that I had to be there, in that village, in that room with a bunch of strangers. Why couldn't I be with my parents in the north? I felt like an outsider and of course my pregnancy didn't help me cope with things any better. As my belly grew bigger, I became more restless and more agitated. The cold burns on my skin were hurting me a lot and going out in the garden to wash the dishes seemed like a challenge. With Soltan being sick, I carried out the most chores. The prolonged flu made Soltan weak and fragile and I tried to nurse her any free moment I could get.

Each day we tried to do some regular activities, such as knitting, to keep ourselves busy. Men went back to the city once a week to bring supplies including: canned food, candles, medications, groceries, clothing and batteries for our flashlights. But when the ominous night unfolded its darkness and widened itself up over the village, we sat inside the room as our shadows danced on the walls with every tremble of the candlelight.

Most of the time I sat there quietly and rarely got engaged in any conversation. I thought about how my life had turned out the way it had and wondered if any of it was really up to me. I couldn't find myself so much at fault. I blamed fate, and I called myself a victim of our own culture and the world's political affairs. Surely, I lived a life I could never get used to; inevitably, I had no other choice but to live it. We were people in exile, who in so many ways lived and experienced the terror named "war."

From that village, we could see the Iraqi airplanes that flew toward Isfahan. They had to fly over the village in order to get there. So, every time we saw those Migs, we knew our city was going to be bombarded in the next few minutes. I felt pain at the sight of those planes that passed us by. I knew they would never bomb the village. I knew that we were safe there because they wanted bigger and more important targets. Isfahan, the city I called home, had been one of the main targets since the first air attack. I felt bad for the people who were still living there.

Finally, during those days of retreat and flee, on a cold day in Feburary, my daughter was born in that very room with the help of an old midwife from the village. But soon after she was born, something went wrong and I started to bleed abnormally. Manoochehr and his brother rushed me to the closest clinic where a doctor saved my life by performing a hysterectomy. Later on, after a long period of recovery, I thought about the fact that I couldn't have any more children. It didn't bother me much, because I already had my daughter. Manoochehr and his family didn't take it as well as I did; because I hadn't given birth to a boy and most importantly, I couldn't ever give them a son to carry on the family legacy. After the surgery, Manoochehr didn't talk to me for a long while and when he finally did talk, he blamed me for the whole thing. He told me that my prayers to have a girl had been answered.

"*Perhaps she did some spell,*" *Mom Taban added. I didn't care what they thought about me; all I knew was that as a mother I had a big responsibility on my hands.*

I named the baby Sepideh; it meant "dawn." I chose that name in memory of all those sunrises Pooya and I had witnessed together. Luckily, and even more surprisingly, Mom Taban didn't have any objection to the name I picked.

"*The hell with the name, I'm too angry to worry about a name,*" *she told Manoochehr when he wanted to know her opinion. Manoochehr didn't make any comments on it either, he just walked out of the room.*

After giving birth to my daughter, all I could think about was how to protect her from harm. The first time I held Sepideh, I looked into her eyes and I knew that no one would control her life but herself. As God was my witness, I swore that I would do anything to change things around for her. I couldn't let her destiny be anything like mine. My daughter had to have a better fate; I didn't know how to change things around for her, but I remained determine to find a way.

A year later, the war subsided and we returned to our city. The town I knew didn't exist any longer. The streets didn't look familiar anymore. Everywhere I looked, I saw the wreckage of buildings. Dust and debris covered everything. My parents' house had been destroyed, so was Taban Market. Almost every place I knew had been hit. So many people had been killed and I can't tell you how relieved I felt that my parents had fled to the north long before and didn't remain in Esfahan. However, I missed them so much and I wanted them to see Sepideh.

On our way to Manoochehr's house, I couldn't help but hope to see it safe. After all, I lived there and I needed a place to raise Sepideh. I remember when our car turned on Darvaze-Shiraz and headed up the hill; I held my breath and closed my eyes. Just a minute more and we were going to be on top of the hill. I didn't dare to look. Finally the car stopped, and I opened my eyes and let out a deep breath as I saw our house standing, unharmed. Down the street was wreckages of a few houses. I had known those neighbors; We heard that they were all killed. *Of course, the question remained about the safety of that area. All of us wanted to know if we were going to be out of harm's way.*

"I wanted to ask the same thing. How did you all decide to go back to Esfahan? The war wasn't over yet," I asked grandma.

"No, only a cease-fire at first and no one could really know what would happen next, but we couldn't stay in that room in the back of the garden forever, either. So we waited and hoped for the war to end; then later on, the war just ended."

Grandma took a glass of water; she drank some and then continued:

Right before the cease-fire our soldiers were able to push back the Iraqi Army—out of our land. The lands conquered by Iraq were again ours. The fact that we didn't lose the war shocked the world.

"How did Iran manage to win without help from any other country?" the world questioned.

What the world didn't know was that Iran had the will. Iranian soldiers fought with everything they had. They didn't fear death. They didn't need weapons; they were the weapons. Deep in my heart, I felt proud. I never thought that would matter to me, since I hated the war and I held it responsible for the heartache and misery we all experienced. But in the end, it did matter; it mattered a lot. After all, it was my country, my homeland. Well, nobody likes war, nobody likes the suffering it brings, but if it falls upon us by force, we have no choice but to go through it. Then of course it feels better if we come out on the winning side at last.

People started to pick up what they left behind and began to build the city again. During those first days after we returned to Isfahan, I tried to call Shiva in England, but I got no answer. I wanted to know if her family had fled somewhere else. I wanted to know about them, about her especially. I cared for Shiva very much. I went and checked their neighborhood myself and with much relief, I found their house unharmed.

I also checked to find others, other people I knew. I learned that most of my relatives had left Isfahan while they had a chance. But some were killed, and some were missing. My parents called me a few times to see how the baby and I were doing, and of course as usual, I had to pretend to have a perfect marriage. They already knew about their house being destroyed.

"One of Papa's friends called especially to give us the news firsthand," Mama said. She sounded absolutely heartbroken about losing the house she loved so much. Mama also told me that Papa already started his teaching career again by getting a job in a school and they were settling down in Chaloos, a small town in the north by the Caspian Sea.

My life, on the other hand, wasn't much different. Except for one thing, I was different; I had motivation. I had a purpose that gave me a desire to live again. My daughter Sepideh gave me the strength I needed to go on, to live the life that fate had cruelly bestowed on me. She could mend my heart, my daughter. She could easily put a smile on my face, like no other could. I spent most of my time with her and we were inseparable. God knows how many times Mom Taban tried to break the bond between Sepideh and I. But the more she tried, the less she succeeded. Sepideh didn't want to go anywhere with her father or grandmother unless I went, too.

With Taban Market gone, Manoochehr had lots of free time and together with his brother, they signed a contract with a professional constructor to rebuild the Market. The construction had already begun, but it didn't require Manoochehr's presence at the site. His brother did most of the onsite supervision. So, as a result, Manoochehr remained home for the most part and he didn't seem too happy learning that our daughter preferred me to him.

He started to abuse me more and more, physically and mentally. He began to blame me for every little thing that went wrong in our household. Little issues very often led to bigger and more hostile arguments. We fought over almost everything, as he always picked on me.

"It's your fault that Sepideh doesn't feel well," he yelled. "Why doesn't she feel good? I know you did something wrong," he accused me as usual.

"You think I do things to make her sick? You honestly believe that?" I asked him.

"If you took good care of her, she wouldn't be sick, would she?"

"She's not sick; she doesn't feel good because her gum hurts. Didn't you hear what the doctor said? She's teething."

"I don't care what that idiot doctor said. You can defend yourself as much as you want, but you're an unfit mother," he always told me.

But that wasn't all. If Mom Taban became sick, he accused me of being negligent toward his mother, too. It seemed to be always some laxity on my part. I had to be the one to blame; therefore, he could beat me up and make me pay. I remember one night he pulled me ever so violently out of the bed, for me to hear a mouthful of curses, to be pushed to the wall and I didn't even know why.

"What crime have I committed? Why? Why? Why?" I kept on asking as he kept on hitting me. He refused to give any explanation, just as I refused to stop asking the question.

"Why are you beating me now? What did I do?" My arms shielded my head.

"Didn't I order you to take care of mother while she is sick?"

"Yes, and I swear to God I did, I am taking care of her."

"Why doesn't she have an extra bottle of water at her bedside?" He held my arms. His fingers were pressing hard on my flesh.

"I did put everything at her bedside, water, too."

"You careless woman, you left only one water bottle for her. She had to get up for more water but got dizzy and fell."

"Oh God, is she..." I started to say with fear.

"Thank God she's okay now," he interrupted me. "But I'm warning you, Fariba, there better not be a next time. Do you hear? Can't you do anything right?"

"You're right. I'm sorry," I told him just to get him off my back as I always did. I had always apologized and gave in; hoping that would eventually calm him down, but I couldn't have been more wrong.

His behavior grew more violent with each day that passed; he loved to abuse me. He didn't want me to feel good about myself. He used to say that I brought bad luck as he repeatedly battered me.

Come to think of it, now I realize that his behavior toward me wasn't about Sepideh and I bonding. Maybe he had known in his heart that I never really loved him. Or perhaps it originated from the fact that I couldn't give him a son. Maybe it was a learned behavior; maybe someone had abused him as a child. Sometimes I wondered about how he behaved. In any case, whatever may have been the reason; it's all over now, isn't it? Only the memories of it have sunk deep into my heart." Grandma sighed.

Two years had passed by since we came back to our city, and during that time I never heard from Shiva, nor saw my parents. I talked to them, of course, on the phone. Mama told me my sister Ferry was getting married and she wanted me to be there. I felt so excited and wanted to go. I knew I had to ask Manoochehr for permission.

"My mom has invited us to my sister's wedding and I would like us to go. What do you think, Manoochehr?"

"No. We can't go."

"But why? You know I haven't seen my family for a long time. I miss them Manoochehr."

"We're your family now. My mother is sick, you can't leave now, end of discussion."

Manoochehr didn't want me to go, because his mom had a cold. I had to stay to take care of her. To me, that didn't seem fair, but then again in my life nothing seemed to be. I didn't argue with him on that subject. I really, really grew tired of the abuse; all because I had a different opinion about matters. So, I didn't go and missed the opportunity to be at Ferry's wedding. Only God knew how I wanted to be there, to see Mama and Papa again. To see Ferry as a bride, to see how grown Zina and Zaffa were. Not having a voice as an individual and not being heard had its own side effects. The seed of resentment toward Manoochehr and his family that had been planted long before in my heart started to root deeper and deeper inside me.

To make matters worse, almost a year later in the spring, Manoochehr decided to marry again. In order for a man to marry another woman, the first wife had to sign a consent or agreement. Some women agree to that because they don't know any better. Somehow they thought that's the way things were. I, on the other hand didn't want that, not for my own sake, but for Sepideh's. I didn't want her to become a forgotten child once he started to have more legal children, especially if they were boys. I knew Mom Taban stood as the mastermind behind his new idea. Naturally, I told him I wasn't going to sign an agreement. To my surprise, he didn't say anything, didn't beat me up either. Instead, he left and didn't come back until three days later. When he returned, he had a paper in his hand.

"Fariba, come here and sign this."

"What's that?" I asked.

"It's the consent."

"Consent for what?"

"You already forgot? You dumb woman. It's the permission you're giving me to legally bring in a second wife."

"I told you, I'm not going to sign that," I said with anger.

"Don't make me upset, Fariba. You know that I'm going to marry another woman if I want to. Actually, I'm considering four wives. I want to have as many boys as possible."

He had the most disgusting smile on his face. All I could think about was my daughter Sepideh and how he wanted to rob her of her rights by having boys from other women. Under the Muslim law, each boy is entitled to almost double the amount of the father's assets and wealth than a girl.

"No, I'm not going to do this to Sepideh."

He came toward me, held my wrist and twisted it; I wanted to scream out of pain. He pulled me toward the table and sat me down violently.

"Let's just talk about Sepideh, since you brought up the subject… shall we?" He sat next to me and started to talk calmly.

"*Let me see, let's say I can prove to the court that you're not emotionally stable. Wouldn't it be a pity to take Sepideh away from you like that?*"

"*You have no proof that I'm not stable. I have been a wonderful mother to her. You know that.*"

"*Yes, darling, you are absolutely right. It wouldn't be easy to prove that, unless I came up with something good, something undeniable, right?*"

I didn't answer. The tone of his voice scared me a little. I knew he had some plans, but I couldn't figure out what.

He got up and started to walk up and down in the kitchen. His fingers held his chin, as he pretended to be thinking.

"*Oh, I almost forgot to tell you.*" *He sat next to me again before he continued.* "*I've been digging for some information and guess what? I have some good ones,*" *he whispered the last sentence calmly in my ear.*

"*What information?*" *I asked while I tried to remain calm and subtle.*

"*You know, it's very interesting, the things you might find about a person if you dig deep enough.*" *He wasn't whispering anymore.*

I remained quiet.

He continued, "*Do you know I can take Sepideh away from you if I take you to court as an unfit mother?*"

"*And exactly how are you going to prove that I am one?*" *I smiled at him; almost sure he could never prove such a thing.*

"*Easy. All I have to do is tell the court that you're insane and that you committed suicide once.*"

He aimed for the heart and hit the target straight on. I felt pain deep in my heart. He stopped talking and stared into my eyes with a winner's smile, the same nasty smile of his mother. I began to breathe fast and deep. He watched me carefully. He knew. He saw the fear in me.

"*Oh, I see you're not talking back now. What happened?*"

"Who told you that I committed suicide?" I tried my best to look relaxed, too late, I realized. I knew the fear of losing Sepideh already had been carved all over me.

"Never mind who gave me the information. The point is that I have a good piece of evidence that would make me a winner in court. All I have to do is pay some of our friends to testify that they have witnessed your abnormal behaviors a few times. I will tell them that you took birth control pills without my knowledge; depriving me of having a child until I found out and stopped you. I can tell them that you were hospitalized and supervised for an attempt to take your life. I'll tell them that you and your family withheld that information from me, otherwise, I would have never gone ahead and married someone unstable. I will—"

"Okay, okay. I beg you; please don't ever take my Sepideh away from me. Please, Manoochehr, have a heart."

I begged him and cried. I kneeled before him and asked for his mercy. I knew with that kind of information, he could divorce me and take my daughter away. Back then in Iran, the law protected men's rights and women didn't have any. Doomed, is how I felt. With those allegations, I had no chance to stand against him in court. Even without those, he still could take Sepideh. By law, the child always belonged to the head of the household, the father. Unless the woman could prove that the man abused drugs and had been irresponsible and didn't take care of his family. I couldn't prove any of that. Who would listen to me anyway? All he had to do was to mention my suicide attempt.

"Are you going to sign this consent or not?" He held the paper right in front of my face. I got up and signed the agreement. With that, he could lawfully marry four other women if he wanted to and at that point, I didn't care if he did. I just wanted him to leave both Sepideh and me alone.

Chapter 5

A week later, he married a girl a few years younger than me. Manoochehr's second wife Zohreh must have been from a lower class family because people in the middle and upper class wouldn't have approved of such matrimony. They wouldn't allow a man with a wife to ask their young daughter's hand in marriage.

He brought his new wife home and I had to welcome her. When she saw me, she smiled and dropped her veil on purpose; she wanted me to see how young and beautiful she looked. She wanted me to know my days of glory as Manoochehr's one and only "wife" had ended. She wanted me to know that my husband's heart belonged to her. Poor her, she never knew I never wanted nor did I care to have his heart. She didn't know I never had glory days as a wife. She didn't know I never felt like a newlywed, but like a widow from the very start of that marriage.

Although shorter than me, Zohreh had bigger bone structure and looked healthy as a horse. As much as I wanted, I couldn't deny her young, innocent beauty. Her long brown hair, soft as silk, reached the curve on her lower back. She could grab anyone's attention with those inviting eyes. Her seductive lips were full and pink against her

95

glowing fair skin. No wonder Manoochehr spent all his time around her, petting her like a Persian cat. You think that I cared? No; not a bit.

Mom Taban never hesitated to make her feel right at home, and made sure I could see the royal treatment Zohreh got. Zohreh seemed to be on cloud nine and I didn't know how long she had before they would let her see the real side of the family. One thing I may say, though, is for some reason Mom Taban treated her better than she ever treated me in the beginning of my marriage. They started off their relationship on the right foot.

One afternoon, Zohreh came to the kitchen. Soltan and I were busy with chores. We had a table full of raw vegetables to wash, cut and freeze. She pulled a chair close and sat at the table. I looked at her, the heavy make-up made her young face look older. I wanted to comment on her overly made up face, but then I remembered wearing lots of make-up seemed to be a common thing among newlyweds. So I didn't say anything and continued to cut vegetables.

"Soltan, bring me a cup of tea!" Zohreh ordered.

Soltan looked at me and I gave her a signal to obey the order. Soltan didn't like Zohreh at all, I could see that and I knew why. Zohreh never treated Soltan the way I did; I respected her, and had never really ordered her around from the very first time I met her. Whenever I needed something, I asked her politely without having a single trace of an order in my tone. I had never considered Soltan as a maid, but a true friend.

After she brought the tea, Soltan sat down at the table again and continued with her chore.

Zohreh turned to me. "Mom Taban said you can never have children again."

"She told you the truth," I answered without turning my head toward her.

"It must feel awful not to be a complete woman."

This time I looked her deep in the eye, but I didn't say anything and continued to cut the vegetables.

"Well, I don't know about that. Miss Fariba is all woman; although I can't say that for many other people around here," Soltan answered her.

Zohreh ignored her comment. "I think I'd rather die if I ever become barren. How can a man think of me as a woman if I'm fruitless?"

"Don't worry, as long as you paint yourself that heavy, men will look at you." Finally, I made fun of her make-up. I had to say it. I felt impatient with her.

"You don't approve of the way I look, Miss Fariba? Manoochehr says that I look so pretty."

"Manoochehr would say the same thing if someone put lipstick on a cow."

I said what I wasn't supposed to say. I said something that would be grounds for war between two wives. I basically called her a cow. Zohreh got up and left the kitchen, she said she would not sit there to be humiliated by a barren woman and a maid. Soltan and I laughed. But somehow I couldn't stop thinking about what she had told me; being barren and unfertile. I could never experience the joy of becoming a mother again. I could never hold a sweet baby in my arms again. My heart ached with the burning desire to be pregnant, but….

Very soon Zohreh got pregnant. Manoochehr seemed so happy. Mom Taban forced her to eat certain foods, because she believed those foods would turn the baby into a boy for sure. Despite her efforts Zohreh gave birth to a girl. They named her Tala.

The newborn baby kept Zohreh busy and Mom Taban looked sick again. I don't know if her illness had anything to do with Zohreh having a girl or not. Manoochehr spent more time at the newly built market those days and I spent every single moment I had with Sepideh.

Sepideh had just turned four and Manoochehr registered her in a day care center. I didn't mind it, because this way she could play with children of her own age; she needed that. When Sepideh started to go to the day care she seemed more joyful. I felt happy for her. Just *seeing her being content and whole gave me all the happiness I needed. I used to pick her up myself every day. We used to sing the songs she learned as we walked home from the day care each afternoon.*

A summer evening's misty air made the house suffocating and I decided to take Sepideh for a walk.

"Wait, Fariba. I want to bring Tala out, too, just let me get the stroller," Zohreh said.

I didn't answer, but waited at the door for her to get ready. Honestly, I didn't want her to come along, but I couldn't really stop her from going, could I?

Sepideh volunteered to push the stroller while Zohreh and I walked behind her. I didn't want to start a conversation with Zohreh, but she did.

"Manoochehr wants me to have another baby," she said. I didn't answer her and just listened.

"He says this time we're going to have a boy."

I remained quiet and made no comments. I knew the whole purpose of discussing this issue with me was to hurt my feelings.

"Miss Fariba, aren't you bothered by the fact that Manoochehr spends every night with me? Sometimes I feel bad and I tell him he should come to you once in a while. But he says no." Although Zohreh tried to retain an innocent image, I could see the joy of saying that to me all over her face.

I aimed to hurt her, so I said, "I can't believe how naïve you are. How childishly you believe men. Honey, he comes to me in the middle of the night. He always makes sure that you're fast asleep before he leaves your room. You shouldn't really worry about me." This time, it was I who smiled with an innocent face.

Zohreh didn't look happy. She kept quiet, shocked by the new discovery.

To hammer the nail deeper in her heart I added, "To be honest, I never thought that he had this much strength."

I smiled as I watched her surprised, angry face. I knew she could never complain about Manoochehr coming to my bedroom, because she married him knowing that he had another wife from the beginning. Nor could she ask him anything. Men didn't like to discuss any detail of their relationship among their wives.

Zohreh always liked to make me feel like I wasn't a real woman. I, on the other hand, wasn't going to give her the satisfaction. Zohreh was a pretty girl as I said before, but her postpartum weight gain left her with a sense of insecurity. A few times I wanted to tell her she had nothing to worry about. I wanted her to know I never liked my husband and didn't care if he had any heart for her. I would have told her that if she didn't keep lashing me up with my infertility, telling me that I wasn't a complete woman. I would have left her alone, for all I cared.

Zohreh never realized that I wasn't after my husband; therefore, she always had her guard up. She also tried her best to keep the war fully flamed between Mom Taban and I and consequently Manoochehr and I never waved a white flag at each other.

The fall had just begun and so did Mom Taban's arthritis. She talked about going back to stay with her son Mehrdad for a while. She said she needed some peace and wanted to rest and didn't want to fight with a rude daughter-in-law. Of course everybody knew who she called "the rude daughter-in-law." She meant me, and I didn't care. On the contrary, the news of her leaving made me feel happy and I thought she should have done that a long time ago. I didn't know exactly when Mom Taban wanted to move back to Mehrdad's house and I didn't want to ask. I knew from experience that asking too many questions had never delivered good results in that household. I also didn't want them to know how thrilled I felt by hearing that news.

Meanwhile, Zohreh became pregnant again and she had a bad case of morning sickness, which always lasted until early afternoon hours.

J *never really stood up to Manoochehr and his family except for once. On a cool day in September, after spending the whole morning at the gas company for a mistake they made on the bill, I finally picked Sepideh up from her school and returned home as usual.*

When I arrived, I saw a few suitcases in the living room. My husband and his brother were talking in the hallway.

When Manoochehr saw me he said, "My mom is going to live with my brother for a few months. She needs to regain her strength. She has been sick for a long time and she needs somebody to take good care of her."

"Well, if you believe that's best," I said innocently. I couldn't fit into my own skin, and I had a hard time trying to hide my happiness.

"Yes, Mehrdad and I both think it's better," he replied.

I nodded while Manoochehr continued, "But, my mom as you know is very attached to Sepideh and she needs to be around her," he paused to see my reaction.

I didn't say anything at first. I wasn't sure what he was trying to say, but I had a feeling it wasn't good. My heart began to race. I frowned as I waited for him to continue and he did.

"I want Sepideh to go with her, too," he added. What was he saying? What was he thinking? The room started to revolve around me.

"That is absolutely out of the question," I hurried to say with rage. Manoochehr walked toward me and started to talk with his face very close to mine.

"You don't understand. I'm not asking you, I'm telling you," he said angrily.

"No, this time you're the one who doesn't understand," I dared to say.

His eyes widened with fury, shocked by my answer for a few seconds.

"What did you say? What the hell did you just say?" he finally yelled.

"You heard me. I'm not scared of you, no matter how loud you shout. I don't care if Mom Taban is attached to her. She is a big woman; she can deal with it. Sepideh, on the other hand, is attached to me and her feelings are far more important than your mom's."

I could see the rage in his face, but it couldn't stop me from telling him what I wanted to say. I pointed my finger at him. "So, you listen to me and you listen carefully this time: my daughter is staying right here with me, and she is not going anywhere," I shouted. I felt as if my heart would beat right out of my chest.

Of course he couldn't allow such behavior. He moved toward me like a wounded lion and his fist struck hard on my face. I fell on the floor; my nose started to bleed, but I got up. What he didn't know was that I had become a wounded lion, too; more wounded than he. I struck back with all my strength and made him take a couple of steps back. I ran to the kitchen and grabbed a large kitchen knife right before he and his brother ran to the kitchen after me.

"God is my witness today that I will kill whoever wants to separate Sepideh from me. I don't care about the consequences. I will kill all of you, if I have to. So back away, I say," I ordered them.

I held the knife firmly in my hand. I meant every word that I said and they knew it. They could see it on my face and in my rage. They could feel it in my voice, a voice, alien to me, but I liked it. Manoochehr took one step forward, but his brother held his arm and tried to stop him.

"Mannochehr leave her alone," his brother pleaded.

He ignored his brother's request and freed himself off his grip and jumped over the kitchen counter and attacked me. I remember that my arm went up automatically and landed on his shoulder real hard, I stabbed him. I couldn't believe I did that. It didn't feel factual, but what had happened wasn't a figment of my imagination. Capable of violence to the point of harming somebody, I knew I had changed as a person. A complete stranger stood in my place, holding a bloody knife in hand.

When I saw the flow of blood, gushing out from the wound on his right shoulder, I dropped the knife and stood there, frozen. I had blood all over my hand, too. My knees started to shake, stunned with disbelief. It all seemed to be a dream, only I knew it wasn't.

In the middle of that shock, I saw Sepideh standing against the wall, shaking. Seeing her like that snapped me out. 'Oh no, no...she must have witnessed the whole incident. I have to go to her.' With that thought, I went toward Sepideh with all the strength I had left in me and held her shivering little body in my arms.

I wished that I could wake up from this nightmare, but how could I wake up from a reality? It was all real, the blood, the knife and it was I who stabbed Manoochehr.

Zohreh and Mom Taban ran into the kitchen. Zohreh came in first and when she saw the bloody knife and Manoochehr, she started to scream. Mom Taban entered the kitchen a few seconds later and began to weep when she realized what had happened.

"You're mad... You, bitch; you stabbed my son!" Mom Taban shouted as she kept hitting her own head while crying.

Meanwhile, my brother in-law, Mehrdad who went to call for help, came back and sat beside Manoochehr who was sitting on the floor in shock. Mehrdad tried to put pressure on Manoochehr's shoulder to stop the blood flow. A few minutes later, the ambulance took him to the hospital and the police took me to their station.

They locked me inside a dark, filthy, hot room with a narrow bed and dirty sheets that smelled. The sickening dampness of the air touched me all over. The only light I could see came from a crack of a window, very high up, almost near the ceiling. Everything seemed like a nightmare. I couldn't believe what had happened. How could this be possible? Not even in my wildest imagination. I sat motionless on the bed. Did I think about the whole thing? Yes, I did. But nothing made sense. The more I thought, the more I got confused and lost. The whole thing flashed before my eyes. Right from the start, from when I met Pooya, to the time when I stabbed my own husband.

People used to say when we're dying our whole life flashes before our eyes. 'Was I dying?' I wondered for a second. Deep down, I knew that I wasn't dying. No matter how much I wanted to. To die seemed a better option than to be locked up. I had no idea how long they wanted to keep me there. Would Manoochehr have mercy on me and sign my release? Would he file charges and keep me there? Would I have to go to the court? And if yes, when would I stand before a judge? Would the judge listen to my side of the story? Would he be able to feel the agony that I felt, or the suffering throughout those years? Would he understand why I did it? I questioned and questioned in silence.

Chances were slim. The judge probably wouldn't even look at me. He would just sentence me. What would the sentence be? And finally, my biggest and the most important concern, what would happen to my daughter Sepideh?

Those questions spun around in my head like a Merry-go-round. There were endless questions and no answers. I was worried sick about Sepideh. I regretted what I had done. Not because I felt sorry for Manoochehr. Not because he didn't deserve what he got, but only for my daughter, my innocent daughter.

I wished for my own death. I remembered the day that I committed suicide. 'Why didn't I die then? Why? One life would have been lost, mine alone. Wouldn't that be better than this?' I thought. 'This way I destroyed Sepideh's life, too.'

I cried and prayed. I don't know exactly when I fell asleep, but I did. The next morning, the jingling sound of keys woke me up as someone turned the lock. The door opened. Someone whose face I couldn't see clearly stood by the door. A strong light behind him prevented me from seeing anything more than a silhouette. He was tall and had a harsh voice.

"Here is your food." He bent over and pushed a tray inside. A piece of bread fell out.

"Eat your breakfast," he ordered.

He left before I had a chance to say anything. He just shut the door and locked it again. I didn't feel like eating. I remember being very thirsty. I saw a cup of tea on the tray, cold to my touch, but I didn't care as long as it satisfied my dry throat.

I remember the first time Mama and Papa came to see me in prison. The guard took me out of my cell and we walked through a long, narrow hallway. I didn't even know where he was taking me. He didn't answer any of my questions. Very soon we went inside a big room with two wooden benches and a table in the middle. He ordered me to sit there and he left. I felt very nervous and questions were crawling inside my head like snakes. I'm sure I just sat there for only a few minutes, but it felt like an eternity. Finally the door opened and two people came in. I couldn't believe my eyes as Mama and Papa stepped inside the room. I ran toward them. We all hugged each other as if it was the end of the word. I kept looking at them as tears rushed down my face.

"Mama, Mama," I repeated. She'd grown so old since the last time I saw her. Papa also had gotten much, much older. I kept kissing them, sniffing them as if I wanted to breathe their scent into my lungs and keep it with me. We sat down on the bench, Mama and I on one side and Papa sat on the other side of the table, and we talked.

"Papa, can you take me out of here?" I asked with agony.

"I wish I could, darling. But it's not up to us," he answered in a broken voice.

"Why not? Why?"

"What can I say, darling, I wish we could change things," he said.

"I can't believe you stabbed him!" Mama said as she continued to cry quietly.

"He deserved it, Mama. I never told you, but I suffered a lot in that man's house."

"Why didn't you tell us?" Papa asked.

"What was the point of saying anything? You and Mama chose that husband for me. You forced me to marry him. You thought he was good for me and didn't care how I—"

"Please, Fariba, stop," Mama interrupted me. "We wanted what was best for you."

"So, is this the best for me?" I asked Mama.

Mama didn't answer. Her tearful eyes were fixed on me. Anger filled my heart.

"You never told us what was going on there." Papa started to talk. "Every time we asked, your answer was, 'everything is fine.' Do you know how shocked we were when we heard about this?" He sounded so sorrowful. But his eyes were blank. I couldn't read too much from them. Only I remembered a few drops of tears at the corners of his eyes when he said goodbye.

I spent two months in jail before my case was forwarded to the judge and I had to wait to appear in the court of justice, "Justice"? What an amazing word that is. Sometimes in the darkest moment of our lives that word gives us hope and lets us hang on tight. We would think if there is God, there will be justice.

I don't think that way anymore. In the eyes of each individual, justice has a different look. What I call justified and fair, someone else may find unjust and unfair. That seemed to be the case with the judge and I.

The court day finally arrived a month and half later. Early in the morning they took me out of my cell to take a shower, I wasn't due for one in another ten days. In jail, we were allowed to take showers only once every two weeks. They gave me a nice, clean Islamic robe and a new veil. Two guards escorted me to a van with a driver who drove us to court. I felt tense and on edge. I couldn't stop my whole body from shaking. I prayed for the judge to be an understanding man who would believe in women's rights and would see women as humans.

As soon as I entered the courtroom, I saw Manoochehr. He was already sitting next to his lawyer in the first row to the right. Behind them, in the next row, I saw Mom Taban and Manoochehr's brother and of course Zohreh, who wouldn't have missed the show.

My eyes searched for Sepideh, but I couldn't see her in the courtroom. In a way, I felt happy that Manoochehr didn't bring her to a place where her mother would be sentenced. I didn't want her to witness it, although my heart ached for her. From my side of the family, only Papa came to the court that day. He sat silently behind me.

"Where is Mama?" I turned to him and whispered. I hoped that Papa would lip-read, he did.

"Home," Papa whispered back. I wanted to ask why she didn't come. Only I didn't ask.

He looked extremely sad; his eyes were on me. Did he feel guilty for pushing me toward this marriage? I wondered. The impression on his face, the look in his eyes, both told me on his behalf: "Yes I feel a lot of guilt."

His sorrow and guilt, though, didn't make me feel any better. In fact, I felt sad for him. I felt his pain. I knew in my heart that I forgave him right there and then for forcing me to marry Manoochehr. I wanted him to know that, too. I turned my head toward Papa and smiled. My eyes talked to him and he understood, because as soon as I turned my head away, his hand landed softly on my right shoulder.

I put my hands over his fingers for a few seconds. A few teardrops skipped from the corners of my eyes and rushed down my face. I didn't wipe them away. I wanted those tears to drop on the floor; as Pooya's favorite poem said: "for every tear that falls on the ground, a flower would grow and a butterfly would fly."

Finally, the judge entered the courtroom. He didn't even look at me. First, he listened to my lawyer who asked for my forgiveness and then he listened to the prosecutor.

Did I say my lawyer? Oh yes, I only met him a day before the court day. He didn't really know my case and hardly knew me. Only by law, I had to have an attorney. I don't think that my lawyer cared to win the case. His speech sounded weak and pointless.

All I wanted was for them to ask me why I did it and actually care to know the answer. What wishful thinking. No one cared to know the reason behind it all. The truth seemed obvious to them; a sin had been committed by a criminal like me. In their eyes, that was the truth. I attacked my own husband, the father of my child. If they could burn me alive they would have.

As I sat there and listened to what they were saying about me, I felt sick. The room spun around me. I couldn't believe my ears. It was I, who the prosecutor portrayed as cold hearted, insane and wild.

Did I have a say in any of that? The answer was no. How could I? How could a woman speak her mind, her thoughts? How could a woman even pretend that she contained some feeling toward life, her life? What was her life? She couldn't have a life of her own, her own dreams and wishes. The woman doesn't feel; she does not dream and therefore she can't have any wishes. That was the mentality of that world then. I'm so glad things had changed over the years. I'm glad that my beloved granddaughter doesn't have to prove that she's also a human, just like a man is.

～

*G*randma Fariba held my hand as she said that last sentence. Her hands felt cold, and shaky.

"Your hands are ice cold, Grandma! Do you want to stop for a moment? Or if you want, we can continue another time?" I asked her.

"No dear. The memories made me have chills all over, that's what made me shiver."

"Would you like anything to drink, a cup of tea, perhaps?"

"That, I won't mind. A cup of tea is a good idea, darling."

We both went to the kitchen. I made some tea for two and this time, we sat there at the kitchen table. I felt concerned about her, not just because she looked tired, but because I didn't know if digging those memories out from where she had buried them was all a good idea anymore. Although, I felt more eager to know the rest and even more restless to finish, but I couldn't ignore the feelings of guilt creeping inside me. I didn't want to bring any harm to Grandma. She meant everything to me and I just hoped that the recollections would not harm her in any way. It sounded too painful, even for me, just listening, knowing she went through so much agony, so much despair. It was unbelievable. I always thought and knew that there must have been much, much more to her life; but never in my wildest imagination, could I imagine the life she had lived. I voiced my concern of course, but Grandma told me I shouldn't be worried about her, because if she survived living it, she can survive telling it. She held my hand and told me she was ready.

A strong wind made a gusty sound and we decided to stay at the kitchen table where she could continue:

The judge didn't even give me a chance to talk, not the way I wanted. They asked me a few questions with "yes" and "no" answers. The judge called what I did "an attempt to kill." To him, no excuse could be made for what I had done. My actions were not justified, nor fair. None of those years of abuse mattered. He didn't care about the reason for my insanity.

"Time behind bars is what you need," the judge said. "I will put you in jail for a year. This is a very light sentencing. I hope you can realize that we are trying to be very easy on you. You deserve a punishment far worst than that," he added.

Well, what can I say? They took me back to jail. They didn't let me stay a few minutes with Papa. I barely had time to hug him, but I held on to his hand tight.

"Fariba," he called my name with tears in his eyes. His voice broke down.

"I'm going to be okay, Papa."

I didn't want to let his hands go. The guard pulled me away. I walked away slowly with my head turned toward Papa. I looked at him as long as I could, until I couldn't see him any longer. He, too, stood there and watched me disappear into the other room. He had a big arch on his back. He didn't look as tall as he used to look.

I never looked at Manoochehr after my sentencing; although, I could imagine a big smile on his face.

The time I spent in jail is the time I would like to forget the most. The memories are too harsh. There was hard labor and torture. If you think about it, well, you can imagine how that would have been for a woman in jail. Being beaten up a few times a day by guards seemed like a routine activity. As I mentioned before, we were allowed to take a shower once every two weeks. There were times when I screamed out of pain and no one cared to give a painkiller. Any headache or toothache could simply become a nightmare.

But I couldn't call those moments as the worst part. I came across so many women, some young, and some old. Some never talked about their crimes and some did. Among them, I remember a twenty-four year old, Soraya. Originally from Tehran, she had lived in Isfahan since she was ten. She looked pretty in a way, although, a little masculine in my eyes. At first I disliked her; she seemed callous, inconsiderate and cold.

Later, when surprisingly she opened up a little, I realized that beneath the harsh and assertive attitude of hers laid a tortured, abused woman. She had built that attitude as a defense mechanism. We talked about our lives and so many other things.

"I killed my stepfather," she answered calmly when I questioned her reason for being there. The calm in her tone seemed strange.

"Why did you kill him?"

"I was tired of seeing him beating my mother day after day and... and I didn't want to be sexually abused by him anymore."

Shocked and speechless, at first I remained quiet. I couldn't believe a father or a stepfather could do such evil things.

"By the look on your face, I judge that you haven't even heard about things like that before," she said.

"No. I...I never knew that could be! Not even in my wildest imagination."

"It exists, believe me." She gazed deep into my eyes, trying to read my thoughts. I kept quiet.

"So...what are you? A rich woman who grew up in a bed of cotton balls?" she asked me.

"No. I wasn't rich, but I had a good childhood, although I didn't realize it then," I answered.

"Then how did you end up in this hell hole? From a good childhood to prison; it's a long way!" I sensed ridicule in her tone.

"I tried to kill my husband."

"You! You tried to kill someone?" She started to chuckle. "You can't even raise your voice at someone!" She continued laughing.

"*Well, it took a lot of abuse and strength,*" *I said. All of a sudden her laughter stopped.*

"*Were you able to wound the bastard for life at least?*" *she asked.*

"*No…he'll be okay. A small scar maybe, but that's about it.*"

"*You see what I mean? You don't have it in you. You didn't aim well. Me… I killed that son of a bitch, my stepfather, with the first stroke.*" *Soraya giggled.*

"*How long do you have to stay in jail?*" *I asked. Soraya didn't answer; instead, she stopped giggling and gazed into the thin air for a few long seconds and then she got up and walked away.*

"*She's not going to get out,*" *a voice said from behind. I turned toward the voice.* "*They're going to kill her…you know…execute her,*" *a woman explained. Then she introduced herself,* "*Hi. I'm Shaheen. What's your name?*"

"*I'm Fariba. What do you mean they are going to execute her?*" *I asked with disbelief.*

"*What does it look like it means? It means they're going to kill her,*" *she repeated.*

My knees weakened, I felt strange. Shaheen kept talking, but I wasn't listening. I never met anyone who was going to be executed before. A strong sense of sorrow took over and snatched me away. Shaheen's voice broke the chain of my thoughts and allowed me to escape from my lamenting heart. I landed in the middle of something she was saying.

"*…six months,*" *I heard her say.*

"*I'm sorry, what?*" *I asked.*

"*I'm going to be here only for six months, I said.*"

"*Six Months? Wow…. That's not bad,*" *I told her.*

"*No…not bad at all, considering…*" *She didn't finish her sentence.*

I waited a little and then asked, "*Considering? Considering what?*"

"*What I did. I mean, I should have gotten a lot more years. But I knew a few people, if you know what I mean?*"

"Yes…I know," I answered. Did I really know? I could only guess what she meant. I didn't even ask what she did. Still stuck in my thoughts about Soraya, I remained quiet.

~

*T*hose short moments when we prisoners could sit and talk, were the highlight of our days in jail. I looked forward to that. Those were the times that allowed me to forget about my own ill-fated life.

We all had to get up as early as four thirty in the morning to wash up and get ready for our morning prayers. Then we would go to a huge room that looked like a gym. We had to line up and do the prayers. After we finished with the prayer, we were taken back to our little cells where we waited for our breakfast trays. Usually, breakfast was served at six thirty and it contained a cold cup of tea with a hard piece of bread and a small piece of smelly cheese and, sometimes, no cheese, just bread and tea. Other times we were lucky if we got a few crackers.

After breakfast, we did lots of work. We all had to do something. The work included: scrubbing the floors, cleaning the walls or washing dishes. We were constantly beaten up over those chores. The guards looked for little, unimportant things to pick on us.

At lunchtime, we were locked back in our cells. For lunch, we had a cup of soup, which was served at eleven o'clock. Noon prayers started right after lunch. What I looked forward to all day long, was the period right after the noon prayers. Only then, could we sit and talk to other inmates for almost an hour before being taken back to finish our chores. That special hour we cherished as a luxury that none of us could afford to lose.

After that, a trip back to reality, work and punishments awaited us every day. Those punishments varied. Sometimes the guards gave us a few good lashes or no food for twenty-four hours and there were times when the worst, most unimaginable thing that could happen, occurred. It happened to me, too.

I remember it so vividly—the most inconceivable experience of my life. A month had passed since my sentencing and I was asked to scrub the kitchen floor that evening. While doing so, one of the guards slipped and fell on the wet floor that I had just washed. A few people started to laugh. As their laughter grew, so did the guard's fury and rage. All hell broke loose; he got up and started to kick me over and over. He hit me so much I thought my body would come apart if he continued for another second. Well, he didn't stop for another fifteen minutes and my body took it and didn't come apart as I thought it would. The guard threw me back to my cell and of course I knew that I would sleep while starved. My body ached and I cried. I couldn't sleep, was it the physical pain? Or perhaps the emotional wounds that didn't let me sleep. I tossed and turned the wreckage of my body for a few hours and then around three o'clock in the morning, the door opened and four men came in, having the nastiest smiles on their faces. Immediately, I got up and sat straight on my bunk bed, shivering, fearful and helpless.

One of them came and sat beside me, he started to touch my face, ignoring my plea for forgiveness. All of a sudden, he pulled my veil down and grabbed my hair into his fist and pulled me down on the bed. That night, despite my desperate requests for mercy, that group raped me violently, pointlessly.

They left my cell laughing and I…I wished that I was dead. I felt dirty and shameful, violated and crushed. I wished that I had never been born. My whole life danced before my eyes and all the suffering that I had endured seemed nothing compared to what had just happened. I cried no longer; I just gazed into the darkness. I never talked about that to anyone. I thought I could just wipe it out of my memory. But as you can see, no eraser could delete it from my memories and it is as vivid as yesterday.

After that, I knew what all those noises were all about, all those pleadings, screams and laughter that I heard some nights from far distances. I came to understand another ugly truth behind closed doors. Those sort of things went on almost every night. It was the reason behind the question I asked so many times and had received no answer up until then; the question of "Why are some women fine one day and gaze into empty space the next?"

At times asking God to take my life became my most favorite prayer of all. If only God would listen. But then again, why would God listen to anything I wished for? He never did, or so it seemed.

So many times I called Pooya's name or I dreamed of Sepideh. I wanted God to take me away, so I could fly high and join Pooya. My daughter, the one who always made me stop thinking about death, became the sole reason behind my survival. She gave me hope and the will to live. I lived because of her.

Almost six months had passed since the court day. During which I didn't see Sepideh, not even once. Very often Mama and Papa came to see me; their visits, short and sad, too sad. Neither them, nor I, could handle the pain well. One day my sister Ferry came to visit me. She looked all grown up. She had a child of her own, a daughter. She brought her little girl's picture and I saw how beautiful the baby looked. I saw the joy in her face. She talked about her and I listened. I knew how she felt. I knew exactly how she felt. I remembered the first time I held Sepideh in my arms.

"I feel bad. Here I am talking about my daughter, while you're away from yours. I'm sorry, Fariba. Very insensitive of me, forgive me," Ferry said.

"Oh, no, please. I want you to talk about your life. It's joyful to listen to you." I assured her.

"Fariba, I also wanted to tell you that if it was up to me I would have come to see you more often. But my husband, Ali, he doesn't like me to come to jail to see you. It's not because of you, it's......

"Hush...hush, my darling Ferry. I know why. You don't have to explain anything. I don't want you to jeopardize your marriage by going against his wish."

She smiled and I smiled back. I wanted her to know that I appreciated the fact that she had taken the time to travel to see me.

"Before you go, Ferry, I have a request. It's more like a wish. I want you to promise me something."

"Anything you want, Fariba. What do you need me to do?"

"I want you to promise me that if something happens to me, you will make sure Sepideh will be well. I don't care what you have to do, but do what it takes to see my daughter grow up to be a healthy and happy woman, please."

"I promise you, Fariba."

I exhaled with relief. I had no other request; I felt peace.

"But you have to promise me something, too," Ferry said.

"What?"

"You have to make sure that you will do your damn best to be okay, so you can get out and see your daughter grow up, yourself."

"I promise." But of course, I lied. Not that I didn't want to do that. But I knew it wasn't all up to me for things to be okay.

After she left, I went back to my cell, sat on my narrow bed and just stared at the walls. I had no other wish, no other request. My life belonged to the hands of destiny. I needed to wait and just see what God had planned for me. How did God write my story? How would the story end? How much more could I endure?

Questions popped from everywhere; questions to which I didn't know the answers. It felt really strange, as if watching a movie, only, I was the star in it. The star of a drama called "my life."

I killed the hours of the days under the weight of my deep stare. But the harsh silence of the nights was the thing that killed me slowly.

I spent about eight months there and then one afternoon my lawyer came to see me.

"Hello, Mrs. Taban."

I didn't even answer him. I looked at him, motionless.

"I have good news for you. There have been some changes."

"What do you mean? What kind of changes?" He had my full attention by then.

"Your husband, Mr. Taban, would like to drop the charges and he wants things to be changed."

"He wants me to be free?" I asked with disbelief.

"Well, not exactly free." He paused.

I just stared at his mouth waiting for him to continue. He leaned his back to the bars, took out a cigarette and lit it. He let out a circular smoke as he stood there.

"He wants you to be released from jail, but admitted to a mental hospital," he said calmly.

"A mental hospital!! Why? I'm not crazy."

"I know. But he wrote a letter to the judge and it seems that the judge has already decided to move you from jail to a mental hospital."

"When is all this supposed to take place and for how long am I going to be there?"

"You will be transferred a week from now. As far as how long you will stay there? I should say, until the physician in charge of your case agrees to let you go."

"What if the physician doesn't want to let me go for a long time? No…no. In four months, I'm going to be out of here, in four months. Do you understand? Over there, I don't know how long it's going to be. Please, do something, please," I begged.

"I'm sorry, my hands are tied."

"What are your hands tied with, money? Did Manoochehr pay you, too?" I asked him angrily.

"I'm going to pretend I didn't hear what you just said, Mrs. Taban." He sounded upset.

"So, everything has been decided and done with?" I asked.

"That's right."

I wanted to ask, 'Whose side are you on anyway?' But I didn't.

"I guess money buys everything. He's doing whatever he wants and I have no choice but to accept it?" I said instead.

"Basically; that's exactly what it is." He walked toward me, sat on the bed next to me and said, "Listen…. If you show improvement in your mental status, the doctor will sign you out soon."

"There is nothing wrong with my mental status in the first place. They have to check my husband's mental state," I told him. Anger filled every cell in my body.

"*Look, arguing won't take you any place and certainly wouldn't help your case. I suggest for you to be calm and show some cooperation,*" *he said before he walked out from the cell.*

What was I supposed to do? I couldn't say no. The judge had already signed for my release from jail.

'*Perhaps I should be happy about leaving the jail,' I thought. 'A hospital won't be worse than this. At least they won't beat me up every day,' I told myself to calm my battered nerves.*

Later, I kept thinking and I actually started to believe it wasn't such a bad idea anyway. In so many ways a hospital, even a mental one, could have been better for me. Although, one problem remained: I couldn't be sure I would be out in four months. I couldn't help thinking that Manoochehr would somehow buy the person in charge of my case at the mental hospital and just keep me there as an insane person. The thought of that made me shiver all over. What could I do? What could I possibly say or do to change things? What choices would a woman whose rights had been denied have in a place like that?

Would they at least let me see my daughter once I was transferred? I prayed to God that they would. 'Oh God, how much more could I endure? How much time must go by before they can grant me the pleasure of seeing my own daughter? How long do I have to wait, just to hold her in my arms? I wish I knew.' I wished I could have a little glimpse of the future. I wish I could see what was yet to come, to see tomorrow, and what fate had planned for me. While all these questions remained unanswered, they transferred me to a mental hospital, called Shafa.

Chapter 6

*A*t first, in Shafa, I tried my best to be very co-operative with the staff. Being polite and obedient was a role I needed to play in order to get out soon. I went on with it perfectly, thinking that I could just buy my ticket to freedom by being Mrs. Nice. Playing delightful remained my only way out; at least, that's what I thought. Little did I know that my behavior played no part in the decision making. Later, I realized the person in charge of my case had no interest in releasing me anytime soon.

After being there for about six months, and not having seen a single doctor to evaluate me, I began to panic. One day, I started banging on the door with my fists, screaming. I remember that day, as if it just happened. I remember calling for Sepideh, asking for her, I also called Pooya's name repeatedly. I don't know what came over me; I became out of control.

After that, my days inside Shafa are somewhat blank in some areas. There are parts I don't have any recollection of. I assume it's because of the drugs they gave me. I remember being numb and emotionally empty. I recollect being disobedient at times, but then I draw a blank about what happened next.

There are moments I still remember so vividly, like when the nurses entered the room and injected me with something. Every time they did that, I couldn't feel anything for a long time.

At times, I lost total track of time and I didn't know whether it was day or night or which day of the week it was. After eight months, I became more aggressive and I started to fight with the nurses who wanted to inject me again, useless of course. They always won; they tied me down and drugged me even more with stronger medications.

Throughout that period, only one of the nurses, Azam, took care of me with attentiveness and kindness; the only person who listened and talked to me without prejudice.

As the time passed by, in order not to be drugged heavily, I learned to be more co-operative with the nurses, I learned to compromise.

After being there almost for nine months, a doctor finally visited me for the first time. He came in, ordered some drugs, whispered to some nurses and walked out. I didn't get a chance to talk to him and it seemed as if he didn't care much to talk to me.

"Who was that doctor?" I asked Azam.

"His name is Gilani. I don't like him much; he has no heart."

"Is he my Doctor?" I asked.

"Yes, he is. He's the one who looks at your chart from time to time and orders your medications."

"But he didn't talk to me at all. How is he going to evaluate me? How is he going to sign my release?"

"Well, I don't know much, but I know that he works under another doctor. He has to report to him. He can't discharge anyone without getting the okay from the other one first."

"What's the name of the other one?" I asked.

"Dr. Sohrab." Azam said.

"Sohrab? Sohrab. Why did that name sound so familiar to me?" I wondered. I couldn't recall.

"Would Dr Sohrab come to evaluate me?"

"He never comes to see the patients. He reads Dr Gilani's reports and decides whether or not a patient should be released," Azam explained.

My silence made her feel sorry for me.

She looked at me and added, "Why don't you stop thinking for a minute? Don't be sad, come and sit here. I want to comb your hair." It was her remedy to release tension and it always worked.

I surrendered to Azam's antidote. She started to comb my hair and I just sat there on the chair with my head tilted back. My hair hung down freely as it bounced back each time the comb released itself from the caress of the strands.

~

*M*y so-called husband never came to visit me himself, nor did he let anyone bring my daughter to me. My family visited a few times. But they couldn't really do anything for me. I recall when my parents came to Shafa.

"Mama!" I jumped into her arms.

She put her arms around me. Papa did the same.

"Oh child, my poor, poor Fariba what can I say." Her tears rushed down her face as she talked. "We begged Taban's family to drop the charges when you were in the jail. We didn't know that… that he would put you in here and…." Mama stopped talking and started to cry.

"Manoochehr told the judge that you're crazy and need to be locked up," Papa finished Mama's sentence. "We believe that he might have bribed the judge, too," he added.

"I think he bribed the doctor also, the one in charge of my case," I muttered "What are you saying, Fariba?" Papa asked, alarmed.

"Nothing, Papa…I'm talking crazy here. How is Sepideh? Have any of you seen her?"

"We tried; Manoochehr doesn't let any of us see her," Papa said as Mama continued to cry.

"Ferry got in touch with them so many times and asked to see Sepideh, but they denied her request every time," Papa added.

"So this is it? I'm going to spend my life here, like a crazy person, not being able to see my daughter again?" A deep silence conquered the room and my questions remained unreturned.

"You know, back then, everything seemed to be different from now." Grandma sighed. "I think I told you this before; men had all the rights to make decisions and Manoochehr wasted no time making all the wrong ones on my behalf. Women had no rights at all." Grandma explained. She paused to think and then continued:

Don't get me wrong, I regret the barbaric act that I did, and I should have known better than to stab my own husband. What can I say? The thought of losing Sepideh to my mother-in-law drove me wild and crazy. I wasn't willing to let them take Sepideh away. I didn't want her to live with that woman somewhere other than where I lived. I didn't think about the consequences of my action and I lost Sepideh anyway. Basically, I wrote my own sentence and Manoochehr locked me in, and threw the key away. I felt that the world had turned against me. Everything, the whole universe had turned against me.

I lost Pooya, Sepideh and my freedom as well. Nothing else mattered anymore. Most nurses thought I deserved what I got, 'How dare a woman attack her own husband,' I heard them whisper so many times. Some felt pity for me and some shook their heads as they passed by. My heart took pictures of all those moments. The rest remained as a pure void, empty space. I tried to relive my life through the vague memories. The drugs made it all cloudy and unclear in some parts. But the memories of Pooya and Sepideh were still strong; so strong, that I didn't even need pictures of them to look at. They were always there with me, wherever I went; right there in the room, in the garden, in the form of a cloud in the sky. I had endless dreams about the two. The dreams never stopped. I held onto those memories when I could still feel. Those reminiscences, those were all I had left.

Most of the day, I sat in a wheelchair. We weren't allowed to walk or wonder around the place. There were so many other women like me, some young, and some old. Many had hope still, and some had given up. *Through their eyes, one could see so much of their untold stories. I used to stare at them while they gazed at me. Most of us never talked. Either too painful to talk, or we just simply preferred the world of silence. It may sound funny, but the silence which used to bother me at night in the jail, gave me a sense of calm and peace over there in the hospital; a sense of tranquility, to draw back, to retreat and be left alone in my own world and I wanted that. I wanted to be left alone.*

Most of those women, except for a few, didn't look insane. How many of them were really sick? I always wondered. Did any of them live a life like mine? Was it true that most of them were wrongly tagged as crazy? At least that's what I thought and I felt sad looking at them. They were part of me and I was a part of them, after all. So difficult to think about those women and the reasons for which why they were there. Surely, there were so many women like me who weren't really sick but victims of society's ignorance. It must have been a tough thing to be there every day and see all that, and I asked Azam one afternoon.

"*How can you work in a place like this? I mean, you must see so many wrong things, all these poor women here, doesn't it bother you?*"

Azam stopped detangling my newly washed hair, thought for a moment, and said, "Of course it does. But I think I can help them. They need a friend here. I become that friend."

"*I guess you're right. I'm glad you're here. You certainly have made me feel better so many times. You have pulled me out of the darkest moments," I told her.*

She smiled but didn't say anything.

I continued, "You know I really don't want to ask any of them about their lives. I'm afraid to ask. I can't handle any more heartache. I still think about Soraya. I can't erase her from my mind."

"*Who's she?" Azam asked.*

"*Someone I met in jail, before they sent me here."*

"*How long did she have to serve?"*

"*They weren't going to let her out. She was waiting to be executed, while being a victim herself; the victim of a crime far more awful than what she committed.*"

"*Just like you,*" *Azam commented.*

"*Just like me, except I won't be executed,*" *I answered.*

"*Try not to think about these things, Fariba. Don't you have enough problems yourself? Everyone has a destiny, we can't change that,*" *she said. I remained quiet.*

"*Let's change the subject, shall we? No more sad things, only good stuff, okay?*" *She added,* "*My God, Fariba, what did you do to your hair? I've never seen it this tangled up before. Anyway where was I? What I was saying?*"

"*You said let's talk about good stuff. Although, I don't believe there is any.*"

"*Oh c'mon, Fariba, stop it. So many good things, beautiful things are left in the world still.*"

"*So why don't you tell me about all those then?*"

"*Okay, let me think. Oh I know, did I tell you about one of the newest shareholders here?*" *Azam asked with the naughtiest smile on her face.*

"*No, you didn't, who's he?*"

"*Fariba, you should see him. He's so handsome. My God, you should see him.*"

"*What's the point?*"

"*What's the point? Oh, don't be a party pooper, Fariba. There are good things in life, you know.*"

"*I know, I know. You just told me that a few seconds ago.*" *As I said that, I couldn't help thinking, 'I don't even care who is handsome and who's not, not anymore. I know only one handsome man and he lives in my heart, and that is Pooya.'*

Azam had finished combing my hair and started to struggle with the veil. "*God knows how I hate these veils we have to wear,*" *she said with annoyance.* "*All right, it's all set. Are you ready for outside?*"

"*Ready.*"

Sometimes in the afternoon, if the weather allowed, they took us outside to the front yard, to the garden. I enjoyed it very much. I tried to behave so they wouldn't take that simple pleasure away from me. In the garden, the beauty of the flowers always mesmerized me. You know how much I love flowers.

Then, one day as I looked at all those flowers, I saw it. It stood alone by itself at the left corner of the building, right before the main entrance. I couldn't believe it, right there it stood out and I had never noticed it before.

I'm talking about my favorite wildflower, the one I loved so much. The one Pooya used to pick for me. You can imagine how fast I wheeled my chair toward the main entrance. I wanted to pick it and bring it to my room. I wanted to dry it and keep it with me forever. I couldn't see or hear anything else; my mind closed itself to all other surroundings and opened up to the only thing that remained, to that flower. I wheeled my chair toward it as fast as I could and soon I reached there, right next to it. As I bent forward to pick it, one of the nurses grabbed my right shoulder and pulled me back to the wheelchair.

"Where are you going, Mrs. Taban?" he asked.

"I just wanted to pick this flower."

"No picking. The flowers are not to be picked."

"No, you don't understand. This is a wildflower. It would grow by itself. I need that. Please...please?" I begged.

"I said no, I'm going to take you back to your room."

He started to pull me back; I struggled to bend forward just to touch the wildflower. The tip of my finger touched it for a second and then he wheeled me back toward the building. I cried, not aloud, but only in my heart. No one could hear my heart weep.

As he pushed the wheelchair, I turned, and kept looking at the flower as long as I could. A few minutes later we were inside the hallway. I thought the nurse would take me to my room but instead, he took me to Dr. Gillani's office.

"What's wrong? Isn't she supposed to be outside?" Dr. Gillani asked.

"Yes, but I think you should know that she tried to wheel the chair toward the main entrance. I think she wanted to exit the building."

"Is this true?" Dr Gillani asked me as his eyes widened.

That nurse rushed to answer before I could. "Yes, when I saw her she was wheeling the wheelchair very fast toward the door."

"No...no it's not true. I just wanted to pick the flower. You have to believe me, Dr. Gillani. You've got to believe me."

"There are plenty of flowers all around you. A bunch of them are there, right where we usually leave you. But you wanted to pick the one near the main entrance?"

"Yes...yes because that one is ver—"

"Save it!" He interrupted me abruptly and with rudeness. "I'm going to report this to Dr Sohrab. He should know about your little attempt to escape."

"You have to believe me, I wasn't getting away. I needed that flower. Please let me take it...please just let me take that one. Please...?"

"Stop it. I think your case should be reviewed. I don't think you're getting better. Nurse, would you please take her to her room."

"No, no...no please don't take me to the room. I want to be in the garden. No...no...no," I yelled and cried, this time I cried aloud. I acted like a lunatic and of course I made my case worse. I did that to myself once more. I didn't know why I acted so stupid, so immature. I wasn't supposed to lose my control, yell or cry. That only showed and proved I couldn't be trusted.

They took me back to my room and left me there. I sat on the bed and cried some more. After a while, I became quiet, separated from the universe and connected to a chain of disconnected thoughts. Physically, I remained there, frozen; but mentally, I flew far, far away. I remained inside my own obscure world, a world unfamiliar. Still deep into my own sphere, Azam came to see me. Her voice popped the bubble in which I floated and dropped me back in the harsh reality of the room.

"Hi Fariba, I've decided to take my break," she said as she walked toward me. I remained quiet. Azam stopped by the bed and looked at me deeply as if she wanted to see what had gone through my head.

Her mind search didn't take long; she continued to talk almost immediately. "I was sitting with a patient in the hallway and I saw what happened to you today, poor child."

She walked back and sat on the chair by the window. "It's a shame what he did, sending you back to the room like a punished kid." She paused and looked out the window. "If you ask me, someone should put him in a mental institution." She sighed.

Quietly, I listened to her as she continued. "I have seen how he treats patients, sometimes I feel so bad for them; he never listens. Even that young gentleman today, he tried to talk to the doctor; he defended you, you know."

"Who defended me, what are you talking about? Only the doctor and that damn nurse were in the room with me…plus, no one has ever defended me in my entire life. Except for one person, but that person is dead; I have no one to defend me now."

"No child, you're wrong. Remember I told you about that handsome shareholder?"

"No. I don't remember," I answered, annoyed.

"Yes, I mentioned him before.… Well, anyway, he went to Dr. Gilani after they took you away. I got up and wheeled my patient closer, close to the doctor's office. The door was halfway open and I heard everything. You should have heard what he said to Dr. Gilani."

Just for the sake of our conversation, I carelessly asked, "What did he say?"

"He asked questions about you, he wanted to know who you were and why you were taken back to the room and so many other things. I'm telling you, he defended you as if—"

"Great, a shareholder had to defend me?" I interrupted her. "How marvelous, splendid. I can't sleep tonight out of joy. Groovy, isn't it?" I said with ridicule and laughed.

Azam didn't laugh and kept quiet; the expression on her face made me feel ashamed of how I responded to her.

"I'm sorry, Azam. I didn't mean to eject the importance of what that guy did for me. I just…I don't know, I've been here too long and…and I can't look at things positively anymore. I—"

She stopped me from talking. "I understand why it doesn't mean anything to you. You think, what the hell can a shareholder do to change things? Nothing will change, right?"

Azam paused, but didn't really wait for an answer, she added, "Just try to keep hope somewhere in your heart, lock it in and throw the key away. You don't have to think about hope, but keep it inside you. Someday it may find its way back to the surface, to show you the way."

"You're right…you're absolutely right. Let me listen. Tell me what the doctor told him? Didn't he say that I'm a lunatic and he shouldn't worry about someone like me?" *I asked.*

"Something like that, but the young man told him that he should have at least tried to talk to you to understand your point of view, to relate to you better."

"He told him that? Who is this guy? I mean, what's his name?" *I asked curiously.*

"Never mind his name, someone told me his name, but I forgot. But listen to this, the doctor told him: 'With all due respect, sir, I don't think you should involve yourself in the medical problems of the patients,'" *Azam quoted.*

"The handsome guy said: 'I know that I have been here only for a very short time, but I noticed one thing, these patients need someone who can listen to them. They're not here just to be drugged or not to feel.. They're here to be helped and cured.'

"'That's why the doctors are here and that's what they've been trying to do,' Dr. Gilani answered and then, he told the young man that he was too young and too new, with no medical knowledge to understand these patients.

"But the guy didn't want to let it go and he said, 'To understand people's feelings doesn't always require a medical degree, sometimes all *it needs is one person to open his or her heart and listen. I have been spending time with them, talking to them and—'*

"*The doctor stopped him from talking, and told him that they all knew he had been devoting his time and energy to this institute, and he had seen him spending time with patients.*

"*'To be honest,' he said to the guy, 'you're the first shareholder to show so much interest in the patients' well being. We appreciate all your effort and the fact that you care so much, but please leave the medical decisions up to the medical personnel.' Then Dr. Gilani left the room.*

"*You should have seen his face, red with rage, it boiled his blood.*" *Azam smiled. "That young man annoyed him, but you know what? I felt so happy for what he told the doctor. Someone should have told him long ago that it's necessary to have genuine compassion for people.*" *Azam stopped for a moment to listen to the noises coming from the hallway.*

I remained quiet.

"*I don't think Dr. Gilani takes criticism well.*" *Azam paused again to think about the comment she had just made as if she wanted to confirm the truth in it.*

I took the opportunity to ask, "That guy, the shareholder, I mean, he said all that to him, all because of me?"

"*I'm telling you, that's what he did, dear.*"

"*It's odd, isn't it?*" *I said with a low voice.*

"*What is?*" *Azam asked.*

"*He genuinely cares so much about the patients.*"

"*Oh yes, he does; he cares. He has been here about six months or so and I have seen him with patients. He seems so passionate. I wish I could date him,*" *Azam winked at me and smiled.*

"*But, Azam, you're married!*" *I told her.*

"*I know, I know. I'm just dreaming. There's nothing wrong with dreaming, is there? I mean, I'm just married.*" *As she talked, she got up and went toward the door. "Not dead, for God's sake.*" *She winked again and left the room.*

She left me thinking about that nice guy. Who was he, and why did he care? I guess being neglected for so long, I couldn't believe people could still care. Soon, I forgot all about him and remembered the flower, the doctor accusing me of running away, how awful I felt, how much I hated this place and how much I wanted to have that flower. With those thoughts, I tried to sleep; my favorite way out of all those miserable days and lonely nights.

The next day Dr. Gilani came to visit me. Still in my room, I waited to be taken outside. "Mrs. Taban," he called me, reminding me how much I hated that name. "We were going to evaluate your case; we thought you had progressed in a good way." He paused. I remained quiet.

"But as you know yourself, your behavior yesterday, proved us wrong and—"

"Oh please," I interrupted him. "If you just listen to what I have to say, you'll see that I didn't want to escape. That wasn't my intention. You have to believe me," I told him in despair. My eyes were begging him to listen.

"Please don't interrupt me again, Mrs. Taban," he told me. Predictably, he didn't read what my eyes begged for; he continued, "As I was saying, your behavior made us change our minds. We are not going to give you a good evaluation. You should know that you're here for a reason and it's for your own good. We can only let you go, if we see that you are no longer a danger to yourself or to anybody else."

"But I'm not. You see, I would never harm anyone."

"Regrettably, this is not our conclusion at this time.... As for going outside is concerned, I wanted to eliminate that activity, but I changed my mind. You can still enjoy that, but you'll be fully restrained," he said as he walked toward the door.

"Restrained? What do you mean, 'restrained'?" I asked, alarmed.

He didn't answer my question, as if he didn't hear me. He reached for the doorknob, but right before he opened the door, Dr. Gilani turned around, paused for a second and said, "I strongly suggest that

you think about the consequences of your actions before you do them."
Then he left the room and closed the door behind him.

"But you never tried to listen to me," I screamed in the empty
room after he left. "Why can't you listen to me? Does anyone want to
listen to me?" I yelled and cried. No one answered me, no one heard,
or if they did, no one cared.

Just like any other situation I had been through, I needed to get
used to it. I had to get accustomed to the idea of being restrained and
that's exactly what I did. Sometimes, my surviving mechanism amused
people, including myself. It was amusing how my mind attuned itself
to whatever came along next so I could survive. Therefore, I got used
to the fact of being limited physically. I couldn't wheel the chair any
longer. I could only stay in the same spot, where they left me until
they took me back to my room at the end of the day. I always asked
them to position the wheelchair in a certain way, so I could see the
flower perfectly.

Whenever Azam took care of me, she made sure to place the
wheelchair in the direction in which I wanted. You see, only she
understood the importance of being connected to the past, no matter
how small or how big the connection. She knew how memories, good
memories, would enable someone like me to cling to her last drop of
sanity. But most nurses didn't see that, didn't understand and they
didn't care much.

I never understood what harm it could possibly do, if they were
more receptive to patients' feelings. I mean, besides medicating
patients and doing their jobs by the book, didn't they possess a heart?
A heart that would yell: 'Stop and look deep into this person's eyes,
what do you see?' And if they did own a heart, which color covered its
chambers? And what was it filled with? Because, I believed that, no
matter how white people's attire, it could never conceal the shadow of
a heart filled with darkness. But, could I argue? No, because I could
never win. Could I pray and ask God to give them a heart? No, even
God seemed to be nothing, but a vague word those days. My faith
in God faded into something of the past. I wanted to believe again,

I wanted to have faith. But not very much faith lingered in me, until....until a miracle happened.

It happened ten months later, on one autumn afternoon in November. The sun glittered and its pleasant rays shone on the entire garden. I sat in the wheelchair in a corner, feeling somewhat happy; Azam had left me in a good spot. Floating deeply into my memories, that autumn afternoon had a soothing effect on my lamented soul. My eyes still on that wild white flower as I sat there and continued to swim in the ocean of my thoughts.

A man passed by, I especially noticed him because of his familiar cologne, too familiar not to detect. I didn't see his face. I could only see his back as he walked and passed me by. Tall, wide shoulders and brown hair, somewhat muscular, he reminded me of a Roman God. My eyes just followed him. He went all the way toward the main entrance. I thought he would exit, but he didn't, He stopped. He stood right there, by my wildflower; he stood next to it. I could only see his back. He bent over the flower; my heart started to beat fast; my eyes fixed on the flower.

'What is that man about to do?' I asked myself. 'Please don't pick my flower. Please don't.' I wanted to scream. I thought I did, but no voice came out of my throat.

As I watched him in horror, he picked the flower. I felt my heart surge as it tried to explode out of my chest. 'Why? Why did he pick that one? That was mine. It belonged to Pooya and me.' I closed my eyes, didn't want to see more. No point in looking at the vague empty space where my flower had stood ever so beautifully a minute before. I don't know exactly for how long I kept my eyes closed; maybe a minute or two, perhaps less. Then I heard him.

"Allow me."

His cologne, so familiar and... his voice,... my God,... the voice,... the voice was...it was.... I opened my eyes.

"Hello, my dear Fariba," Pooya said as he stood beside me to offer the wildflower. It was my Pooya, my flower. Just like before. Just like those days in the past. Was I dreaming? What kind of dream? It seemed so real. Was I sleeping? I closed my eyes and then opened

again, still there. He looked at me with his hazel eyes. His eyes were full of tears. I could hear my own heart beating. I couldn't speak, I cried instead. My tears rushed down my face, his eyes became wet like a silent river.

"For every tear that falls on the ground…." he started to sing the first verse of his favorite poem, but it was I, who finished the next.

"A flower would grow and a butterfly would fly."

I wanted to jump out of the wheelchair and hug him, kiss him and never let him go. I didn't want to ask any question. I could ask questions later. I just wanted to feel him, to make sure this wasn't a dream. To make sure my imagination hadn't created this. As real as the sky stood above me, he stood next to me. "Pooya…my Pooya," I kept repeating his name.

"I have missed you, Fariba. I had dreamed of the day when you and I would be reunited again. Oh, my dear Fariba. What have they done to you? What have they done?" He kept looking at me as he knelt beside me. He held my hands so tight. I wanted to put my arms around him; I would have if my hands weren't tied up.

Still in shock, I couldn't talk. I could only cry and say his name, "Pooya…Pooya."

I think to some degree I still couldn't believe what I had witnessed wasn't a dream. I seemed to be fully alert and awake, but then how could I digest what had just happened? I decided whatever it was, whether a dream or reality, I didn't want to let go. I couldn't let go.

Chapter 7

*H*ow do I explain that moment for you, how can I? It's not possible for me to portray the magic and the triumph of that moment, not in the form of words, not in the form of paintings. Nothing can explain.

"Am I dreaming? Am I? Are you real?" I kept asking him.

"Yes, darling, I'm real. You're not dreaming; I'm here, here with you." He kept assuring me, but it wasn't enough. I just couldn't believe it.

My eyes, my ears, were they playing a trick on me? I wondered. Perhaps I'd lost all my sanity. Perhaps.... The thoughts marched in my head, and my mouth let them all out without hesitation.

"Your eyes are shiny and alive like a twinkle of a star. Just like before, the way it had always been. The way I always remembered them." I paused; he remained quiet. I didn't wait for him to say anything; I continued talking like a crazy woman.

"How is this possible? You were dead...you are dead; how is this possible?" I kept on talking, asking questions, feeling bewildered. "I used to imagine you being next to me all the time, I dreamed of you.... Is this one of my imaginations? Why is it so vivid?"

I looked at him with disbelief. "I must have entered another dimension!" Crazy as it sounded, the thought did jump inside my baffled, perplexed head and I heard myself saying, "When I was younger, I used to watch the Twilight Zone series. Did I enter the zone? Did I go into the twilight? Or did I find my way into a land of fantasy?" Twilight Zone! Land of fantasy! I seriously considered those possibilities in my head.

Now, when I go back to that time, I can laugh at myself for thinking that way, but at the time, the "twilight zone" idea seemed logical.

"It's just a dream, I know it.... I—"

"Fariba, listen to me.... Look deeper into my eyes. What do you see? You see me, the real me. I'm here because I didn't die. It has been a big mistake, all of it. I was a prisoner of war, not dead."

"But...but they said...Shiva told me they identified your body."

"I know, darling, I know. The whole thing, the identification of the body has been a mistake. Look, darling, I'll explain everything to you in detail soon, but not now.

"So, if you were a prisoner of the war, then how did you get away from their prison?" I asked.

But deep down in my heart, still thinking about the whole thing as a dream, I tried not to blink; I couldn't, fearing that if I did blink, he would be gone again.

"I was among one of the exchanged prisoners when the war ended."

"The war ended a long time ago, why didn't you come to find me then?"

He sighed. The saddest sigh I had ever seen; I felt its heavy weight of anguish.

"Believe me, if I could have, I would have.... I will explain everything later, darling."

"So you were alive all these years! You were alive!" This time, to my surprise, I believed he was real. I can't explain it. I went through all these thoughts and emotions in a matter of a few minutes; from

disbelief to the thought of having entered into another dimension, then, to the terrain of dreams, and finally, from the land of fantasy to the era of reality and belief. I felt my head spinning, my voice shaking. "You're alive. My God…you…you're alive." Tears rushed down again from the corners of my eyes.

"Yes, and now I'm here with you. I came to find you and I did. You thought I could forget you, my beloved?"

"I just thought…I thought that…I thought that you died and left me." I wept as I talked.

"Fariba, there was not a moment that you were not in my thoughts. You are the reason I didn't go insane in that Iraqi prison. You were my reason to have faith. I had faith because I knew I had to see you again, I knew God wouldn't let me go without seeing you."

"I wish I had that kind of faith, Pooya. I dreamed of you so many nights in my sleep and I daydreamed about you when I was awake. But faith…I lost faith when I thought I lost you. I didn't know how to pray anymore. I didn't think God would listen."

"You shouldn't have, you shouldn't have lost faith. Without faith I could never regain my strength. Without faith, I could never have found you."

"How did you find me?"

"That's a very long story. I will tell you all about it later. We have so many things to discuss, so much to catch up on. But I don't want us to talk much more now. I don't want to attract people's attention toward us, do you understand?"

"Yes, darling; yes, I understand."

I couldn't take my eyes off of him, just as I couldn't stop my tears from pouring out. I stared at him like there was no tomorrow; it was impossible not to look at him.

"Don't cry, my darling. Aren't you happy?" Pooya asked.

"Yes, I'm very happy. These are joyful tears, I guess."

"What happened here? Why is Miss Fariba crying?" Azam asked, she walked toward us.

"I think this patient needs to rest. I had the pleasure of talking to Miss Fariba and I'm afraid I made her tired," Pooya told Azam as he got up and went one step backward.

"Yes, I think I should take her to her room, but why is she crying?" Azam repeated her question.

"She said that I remind her of her brother whom she hasn't seen for years."

"Oh, you poor child." Azam looked at me sadly and, without taking her eyes off of me, added, "It's true, you know. She misses her family so much."

Azam paused for a few seconds and then said, "Hey, you finally met this nice gentleman. He's the shareholder I told you about."

Azzam turned to Pooya. "I'm sorry, sir, I forgot your name."

"Pooya Nezzam, and you are?"

"I'm nurse Farahang, but everybody calls me by my first name, Azam."

"It's very nice to meet you. I have seen you and never had the pleasure of talking with you," Pooya told her with his usual kind tone of voice.

"Didn't I tell you how nice he is?" Azam turned and asked me. "Wasn't I right?" Before I could answer, she turned back to Pooya. "I don't know what's wrong with her. It's like she seen a ghost.... I'll take her to her room." Azam then started to push the wheelchair back toward the building. I turned to look at Pooya; he stood there silently, both his hands in his pants' pockets. He watched me as Azam pushed the wheelchair further away. He had a very stylish dark gray suit on. He looked as handsome as I always remembered him.

Of course, it took a while before the idea of Pooya's return sank into my head completely. But once it did, it nourished every cell of my body; it gave me hope and brought life to my tormented soul. He'd dug my body out of its dark, lonely shell and gave it hope and spirit. Reborn again, I felt lively. 'God finally has looked down and seen me. God looked and smiled at me,' I thought. I swear that I could hear God say: "I had never forgotten you."

～

*P*ooya came to visit me every day. I couldn't get enough of his visits. I wanted him to stay all day and never leave. But we had to be very careful not to draw too much attention toward us. He talked to me just as the same way as he talked to every other patient. His visits were short, but we managed to talk about everything, little by little each day. We talked about him, the war and about my daughter and me. We talked about so many things and every time it felt like there was much, much more to discuss and not enough time.

"Whose body was identified as yours?" I asked.

"I don't know, what they identified wasn't a body, but a silver placket, on the body. The one my mother gave me with my name carved on it, remember my placket?"

"I remember."

"A week before our surrender, I lost my silver placket, stolen from me among other things, such as my boots, watch and hat. The person, who stole it is the one who's dead. They found the placket on a burnt body part and, naturally, they decided that the name they saw on the placket belongs to the person who got blown to pieces."

"Aren't they supposed to be certain, before announcing someone's death? Don't they know the consequences of a lie like that?"

"Fariba, my dear, they didn't lie; they made a mistake. In war, certainty is something you can only hope for, but it doesn't always work that way. Unfortunately, there are lots of circumstances where they can't recognize the body. Most bodies are badly burnt or..." He paused. He didn't continue. He had tears in his eyes.

After a few minutes he said, "I'd rather put that memory behind me."

"Sometimes I still think that I'm dreaming, and then I see you, and you're here with me, talking to me, holding my hand and then I know it's not a dream."

"Well, believe it darling, because I'm here with you; I won't leave you, not a chance. I won't go anywhere without you."

I looked at him and my eyes became wet. I closed my eyes and sighed.

"What is it, darling? Why do you sigh? Shouldn't you be happy?"

"Oh, I am happy Pooya. I'm happy that you're alive. I'm happy that you're here at this minute and I am grateful that God gave me this chance to see you again. But..." I paused.

"But what?"

"I wish I was free. Free like a bird, so I could fly with you. But... but they just tossed me here and threw the key away and ....and that Dr. Sohrab. I remember now, he's a good friend of Manoochehr. His name sounded familiar to me before, but I didn't know why. Now I know who he is. I never met him while I lived at Manoochehr's house, but I heard Manoochehr talk about him. I know that he will never sign me out as long as Manoochehr tells him not to. I'm stuck here forever."

"Not if..." He didn't finish his sentence. Instead, he said, "We will see about that. We'll see."

His grip on my hand became tight. I looked at him. His head slightly tilted down and toward left. His eyes, fixed on the floor; he had the most serious look. I could feel that he floated deep in his thoughts. I knew he had a plan, a plan to free me.

~

I guessed right; he had a plan and he explained later. "Everything I've done so far is part of a plan. What do you think? You think it was just a coincidence that I became a shareholder here? All along, I knew you were here, I watched you from the first day I set my foot here. I worked my way up to you without anyone to suspect anything... yes, darling, everything I've done is part of a bigger plan."

"And how did you manage to be a share holder, without having any money?"

"That's the only good thing about being a prisoner of War."

"I don't understand."

"The government, our government gave a big sum of money to all wounded soldiers, including all prisoners of the war who made it back. Basically we don't have to work for the rest of our lives."

"Oh, I didn't know our government was so generous."

"Me neither. But I believe in God. I think everything happened for a reason. I had to suffer in those Iraqi dungeons so that I could later come back with enough funds to save you. I'm going to use this money to help you."

Pooya had tears in his eyes and all I wanted was to hold him tight, but then again, my hands were restrained as usual.

Pooya looked at me and read my mind. He smiled and said, "I know, darling, I want to hold you close, too. My heart aches every time I see your hands being tied up. Just hang on a little longer, my plan will work and I'll set you free."

He got up and left me to go to another patient as he always did and I saw the big smile formed on that patient's face as he walked toward her. Gentleness, a caring heart and pleasantness were all the traits everybody yearned for in that place, and his affectionate heart never did hesitate to offer them what they wanted.

I started to get nervous as he explained a little of his plan each day on our limited visiting time when he could sit and talk to me. Thousands of questions marched in my head day after day. 'How are we going to pull this one off? Was his plan good? Was it going to work? What would happen if it didn't? What would happen to him if they found out? What would happen to me?'

Those questions and more remained unanswered. I didn't want to keep a negative mind, but I couldn't help it. I was scared to death, more for him than for myself. I didn't want them to arrest him and put him away or harm him in any way or shape.

His plan seemed simple, yet I couldn't help being so fearful about the whole event. He talked about this maid who worked in the mental institute.

"She will leave a uniform hidden inside a folded blanket for you after an evening cleaning."

"Remember this is a hospital, not a jail. Security is tight, but not that tight," Pooya told me after he saw the look on my face. His statement calmed me down a little when I thought about it. Shafa wasn't a jail, nor I, a prisoner. Running away from a hospital wouldn't be impossible.

Pooya said he needed more time to set everything up. He said getting me out wasn't the hard part, but what happened after concerned him the most.

"I'm going to issue fake identification cards, driving license, checking and saving accounts in the bank and health insurance cards."

"How are you going to get me a new identity anyway?"

"Don't ask me how; I have my ways and connections."

"Where am I going to live?" I asked.

"That's another issue. I'm going to buy a place."

"What's going to be my new name?" I asked mockingly.

"I haven't made up my mind about that yet," he answered with a tease.

"You don't even have a name in mind?"

"I have a few that would suit you well. I will decide which one it will be."

"May I know what names they are? Can I choose, too?"

"No," Pooya said playfully as he got up and walked away.

Excited, scared and worried, I lived through each day; of course not as afraid as before, but enough to make me lose my appetite. As the number of days decreased toward the final day, fear crawled under my skin and sleepless nights increased.

"What about Sepideh?" I asked him.

"I didn't forget Sepideh. First we settle down someplace safe and then I will find a way for you to be reunited with your daughter." He walked toward me as he spoke.

"My love, I know it hasn't been easy for you to spend this long without Sepideh. Believe me, I understand your pain. Have patience and things will change for the better, I promise." I know he wanted

to hug me and to hold me in his arms, but he couldn't, instead he held my hand tight.

"Just a little bit more patience, my love," he said and then he left. He knew that my heart ached for my daughter; I didn't have to talk about how I felt. He knew it just by looking into my eyes, wet with tears every time I said her name. Thank God, Pooya always gave me the freedom to choose, to talk or not to talk about Sepideh.

G *etting impatient as days and weeks passed by, I couldn't wait for everything to happen and be over with. Finally, one day Pooya came to me. He seemed a little nervous.*

"What's going on? You look worried," I asked him "I am. I came here to say that everything is ready. We'll pick a date."

"That's great! Why are you worried then?"

"It's nothing, just a little case of anxiety, I believe. But don't worry; everything is going to be fine. I will give you detailed instructions soon; meanwhile, you should try to get used to your new name."

"Tell me, what's my new name?"

Your first name would be the same. I thought since Fariba is a very common name, it would not matter if we keep it. Only your last name is changed."

"Are you going to tell me what it is or not?"

"It would be Refah. You are Fariba Refah, not Abari and not Taban."

"Fariba Refah…Refah…Refah…" I repeated my new last name. "I like it, it's nice."

"You like it? I'm happy, one less worry."

"You're silly! Were you worried that I would fuss over a name you would pick?"

"Well, I never know with women. It's very uncertain what a woman's reaction would be over silly things."

"To tell you the truth, I'm happy that you didn't pick a horrible, ugly name; thank you."

"You're very welcome, my dearest."

"So…when is the big event? Why can't it be tonight?" I asked.

"The guard on Wednesdays is a new person, recently hired. He works only two days a week, Wednesdays and Fridays. Last week, he worked for the first time. He is too new to know the faces yet. It will be easy to pass by him."

"How am I going to leave this building?"

"Easy. There is a maid name Fatima. She's a young woman, about your height, almost the same body frame as yours. You've seen her before; she will bring you a set of clean sheets and a blanket as you get them usually each night. Inside those folded sheets is a housekeeping uniform, which is a long white robe with gray trim just like Fatima's. Your veil is also white, unlike the gray ones the patients are wearing.

"Fatima is going to be in your room a little past ten o'clock at night; that is right after the nurse gives you your sleeping pill, which of course you trick her into believing that you swallowed. As you know, the nurse won't be back to check on you until six in the morning. As soon as Fatima starts to change your bed linens you put on the uniform and the veil and leave the room.

"You'll see two linen carts there; one for clean linens and one for dirty ones. Grab the clean cart and push it toward the back of the building and turn right down the hallway. Keep pushing the cart toward the double door at the end of that hallway. That will bring you by the clean utility room. Push your cart near the room; leave it right there and go to the left. You will see an exit door. That exit door will lead you to the backyard. The building service personnel mostly use that door. From there, go to the main entrance where the guard is standing. Act natural and just go out the main entrance. He would think that you are one of the housekeepers.

"As you continue to walk, don't turn back to look at him, just walk. As soon as you get out, make a few steps to the right and you will see a black Benz that is parked there. Get in the back seat. The driver will drive you away."

"Who will be the driver?"

"Me of course; who else?"

My heart pounded just by hearing it.

"I'll be too nervous," I said.

"Naturally; but I know you will be able to pull this off. Believe me, it's not as hard as you think."

"Easy for you to say."

"I observe everyone and everything here. Once you are out of that patient gown and into uniform or regular clothing, no one pays attention to you anymore."

"How come nobody is watching the back door?"

"There is really no need to watch the door; that door is only used by employees. Patients don't know about that door. I bet you never knew that door existed. Plus, even if a patient uses that door, he or she would only end up in the yard."

"So there is neither security, nor cameras for the hallways?"

"No, the only place they watch is the main entrance."

"What will happen to the maid, to Fatima?"

"She will get out of the room as usual, take her dirty linen cart to finish her other duties and will leave at her usual time."

"Then, what will happen in the morning when they can't find me in my room?"

"It would take a while before they check the building, trying to find you. By the time they call the police to report a missing person, you'll be resting in your new house."

"Would they suspect Fatima?"

"I don't think so. She leaves work at night; they will find you missing in the morning. There is no way for them to find out exactly what time you got out, they can't re-run tapes to watch all the activities of the day, because there are no tapes. This is not a major organization with a high tech security system. As I said, this place doesn't even have cameras installed in the hallways."

"Would they suspect you?" I asked with great concern.

"Why would they? I don't see how? I'll be here the next morning, doing what I've been doing; working, helping patients, talking to them and everything else."

"What if they offer money, lots of money to anyone who has information? What if Fatima talks?"

"If she talks, it won't be good for her; it will backfire."

"How?"

"They would charge her for helping you run away. She wouldn't want that. She has two small children and she's raising them all by herself. She can't afford to say anything about assisting you. Plus, she doesn't know who hired her to do this. She doesn't know anything about me and can't connect me to this escape, even if she wanted to."

"Who hired her then, if it wasn't you?"

"That was done through a very good, trustworthy friend. I saved his life during the war. Fatima doesn't know who that person is either; all she knows is his voice and all she has is an envelope full of money, which she believes is from him."

"So you really gave this plan a lot of thought?"

"Of course, darling, what did you think?" He looked at his watch. "I better go. I don't want to spend too much time around you, it's not wise."

He left me sitting there, animated with a series of thoughts. Hopes and fears filled my head. I couldn't sleep that night. Even the sleeping pill didn't work; too much anxiety.

~

*F*inally the big night arrived a week later, the moment of truth. I remember how nervous I felt. My knees and hands were shaking. I knew that I had to stay calm. 'Stay calm…stay calm,' I repeatedly said to myself. All day, either I looked at the clock as the time passed or peeled the skin of my lips. But everything started just the way Pooya explained.

The maid Fatima came into my room about fifteen minutes after the nurse left me. She brought the uniform and I changed into that quickly. When I was ready to go, she sneaked a quick look in the hallway.

"*No one is there; it's quiet,*" *she said.*

"*Thank you, Fatima,*" *I said before I left the room. There were two linen carts there, one clean and one soiled. I pushed the clean cart and started to walk in a normal manner toward the back and then at the end where the hallway divided into two different directions, I turned to my right. I could see the double doors at the end. My knees were shaking, my hands, too. My heart pounded and my neck felt stiff.*

I walked halfway down that hall when, all of a sudden, I heard voices and footsteps coming from behind me. I kept walking with the same pace, not slow, nor fast. Walking wasn't the problem, breathing was. I know I couldn't breathe for a few seconds or more and my heart, my God, my heart pounded as it tried to find a way out of my chest. Two men wearing white uniforms passed me by. Everything seemed to slow down, as if in a slow motion picture. Their voices were fuzzy and unclear to my ears; I could only hear my heartbeat very clearly. They continued to talk. The echo of their voices filled my head and I started to panic. Why couldn't they pass faster? What if they noticed me? What if they see the guilt in my face? Did I look guilty? Guilty of what exactly? I hadn't done anything wrong in the first place. I went through all those questions while the two men walked by me. They kept on talking and didn't even pay attention to me. As they turned to another hallway and disappeared, I gagged for air. 'A minute more and I would have needed CPR,' I thought and smiled. I continued to do what I had to do. I left the linen cart where Pooya told me to leave it and proceeded to the backyard. Once I reached there, I walked a little faster toward the main entrance where the new guard stood at his post. I kept my head down and passed through the big gate and out of the building.

"*Is it over?*" *I heard the guard asking. I stopped and turned toward him.*

"*What?*" *I asked nervously.*

"*Your shift, is it over?*"

"*Yes, it's been a long day.*" *I tried to be calm. I think I did well; my voice didn't sound shaky.*

"Long day, I know what you mean. I have to stay here until twelve. Well, get home safe, good night," the guard said.

"Good night," I answered. I thanked God for the murky night and the veil that kept my face mostly hidden. If he could have seen my face in the light, surely he would have read the fear all over it. As soon as I turned to walk away, I saw the black Benz standing on the right side of the building. Naturally, I wanted to run toward it, get in and say, "Just drive!" but I didn't. Instead, I walked naturally and got in the back seat as calmly as I could. The car drove away. At first I couldn't see the driver very well; his hat shadowed most of his face. The moonless night stretched out and the pitch-black road invited us to go along.

"Where would you like to go, my lady?" I heard Pooya's voice.

"Wherever home is," I answered. Pooya smiled. I saw his face as he turned and looked at me for a second. We were both very quiet as he drove. I don't know what it was; fear, shock, disbelief, or the combination of it all that made us remain quiet for the most part of the night.

Chapter 8

I think both of us were in distress. The fear which had crawled inside me, continued to root and grow. It grew in my bloodstream and my every cell, I could taste it, smell it. I couldn't say much about Pooya, I don't know what was going through his head at that moment, but he looked very serious and alert.

After a couple of hours driving south, out of Esfahan, which seemed like an eternity, we reached another town. I noticed a sign that read: Welcome to Arvand.

A little further down that road, Pooya turned right onto Parvin Street, where our new house stood elegantly. Arvand, a little town lay quietly within miles from Isfahan. The house had an Old Persian structure with arches and multi-colored glass windows. The exterior walls were made of dark gray stones. Two tall pillars stood in front with an arc on top. Too anxious and too scared to pay more attention to the surroundings, I went inside the house as soon as Pooya unlocked the door.

On one hand, I couldn't help feeling relieved by the thought of being free. Yet, on the other hand, the fear of being found and the punishment that could follow overpowered me and I felt agitated again. Pooya must have seen the anxiety in my face, because he walked toward me and held me tight. He told me that everything was going to be okay. I just stood in the middle of the living room and didn't say a word as Pooya's arms remained around me. After a while, my anxiety slowly gave in to a feeling of peacefulness. His embrace assured me peace and calm. I felt secure and serene. "You're safe, my love. You are safe," he whispered in my ear. I didn't reply. Instead I closed my eyes and thought, 'Yes, I'm safe at last.'

Pooya offered me food, but I wasn't hungry at all. I felt exhausted and weary. Soon enough, the exhaustion took over and we both crashed into the soft surface of the bed. In a matter of seconds, we fell asleep hand in hand—so innocently, so peacefully.

Next morning, I opened my eyes. The golden rays of sun had found its way inside from the narrow opening between the two curtains. Its light brought warmth and its glistening glow caught my attention, but not for long, because I closed my eyes again and fell right back into a deeper sleep. This time I dreamed a horrible dream.

I saw myself running through a thick fog, running away from something or someone. The fog prevented me from seeing what lay ahead down the road, but yet, I never stopped running. What from? I didn't know. It didn't seem clear at all. I felt scared and I could hear my own heartbeat. My long dress prevented me from running any faster as it wrapped around my legs like iron chains. I stumbled and fell. The fog seemed a lot thicker there and I couldn't see the ground. Something felt hard under my hand; I grabbed it and picked myself up. Anxious to see what I'd got, I opened my fist. There, in the middle of my palm, a wound in the form of an eye stared right into my eyes. I screamed and tried to wrap the wound with my veil, but the veil couldn't cover it. The more I tried to conceal the cut, the more invisible the veil became and I could still see the eye shaped gash through the sheer fabric.

I closed my hand into a fist to hide the wound and started to run again. I ran and ran until suddenly the fog disappeared and trees, tall trees, surrounded me. I found myself standing in the middle of a forest.

At that point, someone called my name and I turned toward the voice. I saw two people standing across the road, looking in another direction. I walked toward them. The more I walked, the farther away they seemed, and the farther they got, the clearer it became and I recognized them as Sepideh and Pooya. I ran and called their names. When I reached them, I held Sepideh in my arms and kissed her, then I hugged Pooya. I didn't want to let go of them. As I embraced him, a sudden chill ran through my body and his body felt cold as ice. I took one step backward and looked at him. But I saw Manoochehr standing in his place, laughing. I turned toward Sepideh with fear, only to see that she also had disappeared and Mom Taban stood there and started to laugh, too. Manoochehr and his mother both pointed at me while the sound of their laughter pierced thorough my heart.

"I'll get you...I'll get you," he said. His voice sounded strange, more like a tape being played in slow motion. And his eyes, something about his eyes disturbed me and I couldn't understand why. Soon I realized; I open my fist again. That wound on the palm of my hand looked just like Manoochehr's eye.

"No...no...nooooo!" I screamed. I tried to run, but my feet stood still, not moving. Then all of a sudden the forest transformed itself into the same foggy place, empty and dark. I found myself in the same spot where I had been in the beginning of my dream, running through the thick fog again.

I woke up with a jolt. My face wet from tears, my whole body covered with a cold sweat. I jumped out of the bed and stood in the middle of the bedroom.

"Pooya...Pooya..." I called aloud and heard no answer. Terror wrapped its claws around and over me. I sat on the floor and held my knees close to my chest; "I'm safe...safe now." I repeated the sentence over and over, just to reassure myself as my whole body shivered.

I can't remember how long I sat on the floor, nor why I felt that way. It's not always easy to explain emotions. Finally, a calm feeling took over. I got up and left the bedroom, went to the living room and then to the kitchen. I noticed a piece of paper held against the refrigerator by a small magnet, a short note from Pooya.

Grandma Fariba paused and searched through her treasure box. "It must be here. I kept all his letters, even the little notes he wrote. Here it is, I found it." Grandma handed me a piece of paper.

"You really kept them all, grandma?"

"You better believe it, darling. These were very important to me. Why don't you read it?" Grandma asked. So I did, it read:

"My sweet Fariba, you were sleeping and I didn't want to wake you. I had to go back to Shafa.

I wanted to be there as usual, so they wouldn't suspect anything. I made you breakfast.

It's my specialty omelet and you better drink that fresh squeezed orange juice I left you in the refrigerator.

I'll see you after work, darling, rest and enjoy the day."

Love Pooya.

Grandma took the note back from me and looked at it. A long sigh came out of her thin lips. She remained quiet for a few seconds and then she continued with her story:

After reading his note, I sat at the kitchen table and thought for a few minutes. I had to learn how to live again and not be scared. That wasn't going to be easy. I had lots of issues to deal with. My emotional wounds needed time to heal, and I needed to have patience. Throughout the years, I realized one thing about myself; I wasn't a weak person, rather very strong. If I survived those years of turmoil then I could do this. I could heal myself and be happy and whole.

My biggest advantage, having Pooya in my life once again gave me the strength, the will, and worked as fuel for my starved heart. When he returned to my life, he brought back the one half of me that was missing. Although, my heart still wept for the lack of my other half, Sepideh; I only could feel whole if I had both back in my life. There wasn't a day that I didn't think of her and didn't try to picture her face in my head. I knew somehow, someday, Pooya and I would find a way to bring her back. Until then, patience and Pooya's love were my best sources of strength to carry me through.

I sat there for a while and let those thoughts march inside my head. I remember at some point I got up and, for the first time, I felt very curious about the house and started to wander around, observing the place. The house wasn't big; neither small, just the perfect size. The rooms were furnished and neat. Although, it needed some changes for sure, a feminine touch here and there, nothing big, though. 'Some color and some flowers would do the trick,' my mind whispered and my ears heard it.

The garden outside looked just beautiful. I thought I had a little corner of paradise right there in the backyard. The wild colorful flowers, the fresh green grass and the fountains were without doubt, the most beautiful view I had ever seen.

"Grandma, this is the same house, isn't it? This garden that I had loved all my childhood, is the same garden you're talking about, isn't it?" I asked.

"Of course it is, my darling. This is the same house Pooya brought me into that night."

Grandma got up and went toward the window and looked outside. She gazed at a corner of the garden as if she remembered herself standing there in that garden for the first time.

"Pooya and I never changed the structure of this house. The interior decorations have changed throughout the years, such as the color of the walls, furniture and curtains."

She paused for a while and then she said, "I'm very tired, dear; I could use a break. How would you like to have some tea with me on the porch?"

"I would be delighted, Grandma," I told her.

I watched her as she walked slowly toward the porch. She was the woman I had always cherished. But that day, I also realized how proud I felt to have her as my grandma. In my eyes she was a portrait of beauty and strength, a sacred person. Someone I didn't want to lose.

I followed her onto the porch and gave her a big hug. I hoped she could feel all the love I had for her in my tight embrace, and she did. I saw it in her eyes; I saw the twinkle of the tear. I knew she felt my love, "It's the tear of joy," she said. I knew that, too, I felt her joy and I smiled.

"You have your mom's smile, Sepideh smiles like that."

"Really? I thought I smiled like you, Grandma?"

"You do so many things like me. You walk like the way I used to walk. Many of your expressions remind me of myself when I was young, but never your smile. That's Sepideh's smile."

~

I didn't let her continue that day. She needed her rest and I couldn't help being concerned that I pushed her too much. She agreed to have a break. We sat on the swing and talked, just a regular chat like we did years before.

The next day, she got up early and by the time I woke up, she already had breakfast ready. She made me an omelet. "This was Pooya's specialty omelet, the one he made for me on that first morning."

"He taught you how to make the omelet?"

"No, he didn't want to teach me that one. He said that was his secret recipe. But I watched him one morning as I hid behind that window and I saw what he put in it."

"I can see this is a cheese omelet, but it tastes so different from regular cheese omelets. What's in it?" I asked Grandma.

"Sorry, I can't tell. This is my secret recipe now." Grandma winked at me as a nice grin sat on her lips.

"Grandma, did they ever look for you?" I asked as I put another piece of that omelet in my mouth.

"Oh, I didn't tell you that part yet? Well, two days after my escape, Pooya brought a newspaper home. They posted a little article about a missing patient, nothing big. Pooya had told me that it would be an article in the newspaper and we were worried about the outcome if the article should print."

"How did Pooya know what they were planning to do?"

"If you remember, Pooya remained as a shareholder in that hospital and he didn't stop what he used to do in Shafa. He continued to work there for a few years after my escape. So he always knew what they were planning to do firsthand. No one ever suspected him about having anything to do with my running off; no one could make any connection between us to that extent.

"Pooya sat in the room with Dr. Sohrab when he contacted Manoochehr and told him about the escape. Dr. Sohrab told Pooya that Manoochehr became very angry when he heard the news and he wanted the hospital to put an article in the newspaper at the hospital's expense. The hospital agreed of course and they placed an article in a local newspaper about a missing mental patient. I saw it myself; a small little piece with no picture, no clues. We were both surprised as well as happy to see that they didn't even do their best to find me. That article didn't describe me at all. No one could recognize me, even if I stared them in the eye. I can't tell you how relieved we both were.....Darling, are you finished with the breakfast?" Grandma asked.

I nodded. I offered to wash the dishes and when I was done, we went to the living room and Grandma continued her story.

"Let me start back from that very first evening when he came back home." Grandma hesitated. "I'm jumping from one thing to another; I'm losing my way of telling the tale, aren't I?"

"No grandma. You're doing fine…. What happened that first evening?"

"That evening when he came home, Pooya brought me a big bouquet of flowers and a diamond ring. He asked me to marry him. There is no need for me to tell you how I must have felt at that moment; you can't possibly imagine my joy.

"Yes, I know how it must have felt, but grandma, you couldn't marry him. You were not legally divorced yet, were you?"

"No, you're mistaken. Fariba Abari didn't get a divorce, but Fariba Refah wasn't even married. With my new identity, I could marry him and I did. We were married a week later in our own garden."

Grandma got up and went a few steps forward toward the garden and pointed at a big weeping tree.

We stood right there, under that tree, surrounded by all those jasmines and lilacs and got married. The white wedding dress Pooya gave me looked very simple, but elegant. It reminded me of those pictures I used to see in Mama's old magazines, very classic, very sixties and chic. A matching hat was exclusively made to cover all of my hair. He told me that he'd hired one of the best tailors in Esfahan to make that dress a few weeks before the escape. I believed it was so, because he couldn't have possibly found a dress like that in any boutique due to its classic and unique style.

Pooya wore a stylish black suit that made him look even taller. With his gorgeous face and his wide masculine shoulders, he looked like one of those Gods in the fairy tale stories, unbelievably handsome and so perfect. Anyhow, we got married in the presence of an Ayatollah* and two witnesses from the nearby house of worship. I can close my eyes now and see myself the way I looked in his eyes, the way I saw myself through his eyes. I felt truly blessed.

On our wedding night, white rose petals covered our entire bed and candles were burning at each corner of the room. His touch, as gentle as the caress of a spring breeze gave me all the assurances of a pure love. That night, our bodies became one and our hearts mended. I truly felt like a bride for the first time as we shared the magic of a physical love together, a love, so pure and powerful. He made me feel so beautiful, he made me feel like a woman and for the first time, I felt happy to be one. That night became the most enchanted night of my entire life. He remained so affectionate and yet so vibrant throughout

---

*   Ayatollah – a religious figure who can perform the marriage ceremony. (A priest) the night, full of energy, full of hope and dreams. He told me that he wanted to take me to the most beautiful places in the world, places we'd never been before. He talked as gently as he held me in his arms, with so much love in his voice.

I told him that we didn't have to go anywhere, because we were already at the most beautiful place, and I meant what I told him. In fact, I didn't want to go anywhere. I wanted to just stay there in our house together, forever.

Pooya was truly a good man, a good provider, wonderful, kind and very sweet. So many times, I wanted to write a letter to Papa and say: "This is the man you deprived me of. This is the man you disapproved so badly of. You kicked me and yelled at me just to forbid me to see him and yet, this man was my savior at last."

But of course, I never wrote such a letter to Papa because I forgave him that day in court. I wanted to forgive him. It wasn't his fault anyway. He thought just like any typical Iranian father would think. After all, he had only my happiness in mind. All of that belonged to the past anyway. All of it had been a nightmare and I didn't have to continue it by remembering. I didn't have to dream bad dreams anymore and Pooya was there to help me dream only good dreams.

From time to time, I remembered the night of the escape and the fear that I felt during that time. Then, I always thought about the way everything happened after. How clueless that article had been, how no one miraculously ever followed up with that case. I believed that God had helped us in more ways than I wanted to admit. I started to believe that I didn't have to hide from the world any longer. But I needed assurance and only Pooya could provide that for me with his answer.

"Pooya, do you think we are still in danger, should we be afraid? We don't need to tiptoe any longer, do we? I mean, no one remembers it anymore. People have forgotten it."

"We can be more relaxed, but I'd rather be cautious, at least for a little longer. I don't know; for some reason, I can't understand why they let this case go. Why didn't they make much effort to find you? This is a mystery to me."

"*So what if they didn't? You're unhappy because we got away with it so easy?*" *I said with rejection.*

"*Darling, darling, what I mean is that I'm just puzzled by it. Okay…what I'm really trying to say is that we don't have to jump over any little noise, or run on account of any stone that is thrown somewhere. But we should not let our guards down yet.*" *He paused, looked deeply into my eyes and continued.*

"*Look, darling, all I'm saying is that we can relax more, yet, stay wise and keep our ears and eyes open.*"

I didn't say anything to him, but I kept thinking that if the danger was not really over, how could we possibly relax? As those thoughts were dancing in my head I got up and took the dishes to the sink to wash. He followed me; he read my mind because he grabbed my arm and gently turned me back and pulled me close.

"*Fariba, everything is going to be okay. Don't worry. I think the danger is over. Nine months have passed and we're here, safe and sound.*"

As he held me again in his arms, I felt safe. Once again, as soon as I looked into his hazel eyes, I felt secure. Pooya had a magic touch, or was he the magic itself, perhaps an angel, Yes, that's how I saw him through my eyes; the most handsome angel anyone could have and it was I who had captured his heart.

~

*A*s more time passed, I knew that the case of a missing patient turned into nothing more than a forgotten dusty file, sitting on some shelf. Pooya and I were less worried and more at ease. He continued to work in Shafa for another two years and then he sold his shares and eventually stopped going there.

The first few years, I didn't really socialize with anybody. In the beginning, the fear itself kept me inside my shell, but after a while, I remained secluded only as a precaution. I didn't know most of the neighbors. Sometimes they saw me in the garden and I saw them passing by, but no contact was ever initiated. Pooya kept on *communicating with some of the neighbors and the fact that I, as his wife never interacted outside the house didn't raise anybody's curiosity to a questioning point. Not all women associated with anyone other than their husbands and their family. But I should say it wasn't always easy to stay back. Part of me wanted to make contact with the rest of the world and then, the other part of me just felt comfortable with the composure that solitude offered.*

For me, being connected meant reuniting with my own family. I had missed them so much and I believed that the time to get in touch with them had come. I don't have to say anything about Sepideh. My thoughts of her had never left me at any time; her absence in our lives remained as the only shadow that haunted our nights and the only cloud in our flawless blue sky. I knew that Pooya would find a way to bring her back; I had no doubt in that. That wasn't something to discuss, to say whether or not we should do it. We simply had to do it, no question about it, period.

My mind even brooded over Manoochehr from time to time, not that I cared about him, but because of the fact that he didn't do much to hunt me down, to cage me again. He did let me go in a sense, or so it seemed. An eccentric feeling about it followed us everywhere; the only reason Pooya didn't want to put his guard down completely.

Like I said, I wanted to contact my parents and siblings. I wanted them to know that I felt happy and safe. I wanted also to know how they were doing, themselves. 'They must have gone crazy, not knowing, not knowing what had happened to me,' I always thought with regret. Pooya and I used to think their phone line may have been tapped; It wasn't safe to call, so we agreed on not calling. With time, we felt safer and I couldn't wait any longer; so I contacted my family one day. I remember the first call so vividly; I remember it almost word for word. I called, and after a few rings, a voice came on.

"Hello...hello, who's this?" I heard Papa's voice.

I couldn't answer. Emotions wouldn't let me talk. A big fat knot sat in my throat. He hung up. I put myself together and called back.

"It's me, Papa. It's me, Fariba." I had started trembling as soon as he picked up.

"Fariba! Is this you? Is this really you?" He started to cry. We both cried.

"You're back. God brought you back," he said in between the breakdowns of his voice.

"Yes, Papa. Papa, how are you? How is Mama?"

"I'm fine now that I can hear your voice," he said, still howling.

"And how is Mama? Where is Mama?" I repeated. All I got for an answer was silence, an alarming silence that scared me to death.

"Papa, how is Mama; where is she? Are you alone?"

He wasn't talking, I felt heavy. I felt my heart ache, as if it had been crushed in my chest.

"Papa, can you please answer me, please? Are you okay?"

He must have felt the panic in my voice because he spoke. *"She passed away two months ago."* His voice was filled with sorrow.

I froze. Every part of my body became motionless and then my eyebrows came into a painful frown and the tears rushed down.

"Oh God, no...please, no..." I wanted to yell, but no words came out. What did Papa say? I thought I just had a nightmare. I sat on the floor with the phone still in my hand. My knees couldn't hold me any longer. The room started to spin and I was in shock.

"Tell me this is not true, Papa," I begged him as I wept.

"I'm sorry, Fariba....I'm sorry." His voice sounded deep and I kept hearing him in my head over and over. *"She passed away two months ago...passed away two months ago.... Two months ago, I'm sorry, Fariba, I'm sorry...sorry...sorry...two months ago..."* Again and again, my mind replayed those sentences like a tape recorder.

I believed that I sobbed for a while before I started asking other questions.

"What happened, Papa? Two months ago? Why, Papa, why?"

He didn't answer. Again, a deep, annoying, unbearable silence became the only answer I got from the other side of the line.

"Papa, why don't you answer me? I need to know what happened."
I continued to weep. *I knew he listened, I knew he could hear me and I could feel his sorrow and grief, too.*

"Papa, please, I need to know why Mama is dead. She didn't have any life threatening illness, did she? I mean, I never—"
"She became sick after your disappearance." He cut me off.
"Worrying about you drained her..."

I couldn't hear him any longer except for my own inner voice, the only echo that yelled: *'I killed my mother.'*

A week later, I went to see Papa; I had to. It was the first time I traveled under my new name. Pooya wanted to come with me and meet Papa. I told him that it wasn't the right time, so he didn't join me on that trip. At twelve noon, I boarded the Iran-Peyma bus and I reached the city of Chaloos exactly at nine o'clock that night. Ferry and her husband were there, already waiting for me at the bus terminal. I felt very excited and couldn't wait to see them. As soon as I stepped off the bus, Ferry saw me and called my name. I turned around and saw her, too. I ran toward her and a few seconds later, we were both crying in each others' arms. We held on to one another, as if there was no tomorrow. She introduced her husband to me. He seemed like a nice man, although very quiet.

They took me to Papa's house. Zina opened the door. She grown up into a very beautiful young lady. Then I saw Zaffa, my brother whom I used to call 'demolisher'; no trace of demolishing behavior remained in him. He looked all grown up, too, a boy in his junior high years. I painfully noticed the lack of Mama's presence, a sense of void and emptiness in that house. Maybe because I kept thinking what it would be like if she was still alive. She would have been the very first person running to welcome me, to caress me, but instead, she never came to the door. Ferry's little daughter was the next person I met. She ran inside from the back door and went straight to her mother. She seemed shy and looked almost exactly like Ferry. She tried to hide behind Ferry's legs as I kneeled on the floor to talk to her.

"Fariba." I heard Papa's voice from behind. I got up and turned toward him. The arch on his back showed how much he suffered. He

looked sick. I went to him and I saw the tears that shined in his eyes. I wanted to hold him and take his pain away. But he didn't seem to be open to any kind of compassion or sympathy. He had closed himself down. The death of his wife had taken its toll and had crushed him cruelly. My brother and sisters were not as bad. I thanked God for that. It seemed that my siblings had not suffered from fate and destiny the way I had.

Only God knew how much I missed Mama. I closed my eyes and tried to remember the way she used to walk, talk and tried to visualize her as she used to be in my memory. The memories were dull and the new house, a house that I never lived in with her, didn't help me recall events.

Every day I sat with Papa in his living room. Although quiet most of the time, I could feel his sense of relief. The fact that I lived free and had found happiness had comforted him a great deal. I could read that much on his face, even though he had closed up his heart. I knew how hard it must have been for him to talk to me, to the daughter whose life he had ruined, to the daughter he blamed for his wife's death. I couldn't be mad at him for thinking the truth; whether I liked it or not, my disappearance did cause Mama's death.

I forgave him for ruining my life and I wished he could forgive me, although I could never forgive myself. I felt so much guilt. I should have contacted them a lot sooner. I only thought about my own safety. Meanwhile Mama had suffered, dying, not knowing what had happened to me. How selfish I had become through the years. Right there, in that living room where Mama used to live, I wanted to die. I wanted to change places with her. As of now, up to this day, I still haven't forgiven myself for her death.

Grandma reached out to her little box and dug out an old picture. "This is her, when she was in her thirties. Look how pretty she looked. This is your great grandmother."

I wanted to hold Grandma's hand and say she should forgive herself. She should let the old wound heal in her heart. But I didn't say anything. I could see that just like her father, she closed herself to any kind of compassion at that moment.

〜

*A*lthough I stayed there only for a month, at the end I felt collected and composed. Papa and I both needed that time together more than anything else. Three years later, Papa died, too. I was there with him at his deathbed. This time, Pooya was also there.

Moments before he died, he held Pooya's hand and whispered, "Thank you...thank you for saving my daughter and for giving her happiness. Please forgive me for misjudging you the way I did."

He then held my hand and put my hand on Pooya's.

"This is what I should have done years ago." He could hardly speak. He didn't have much strength left, but he made sure that we heard and understood him.

"Forgive me, Fariba, for the fool that I was."

I couldn't stop the tears from falling down my face and didn't care much to stop them anyway; I held his weakening hands tightly.

"Papa, I had forgiven you years ago. Papa, I love you...I love you. I want you to know that."

He looked in my eyes, smiled...and he died.

〜

*W*ith my parents,, part of me died, too; part of me, as well as another chapter of my life. I finally closed the pages of my childhood and adolescent life. It forced me to realize that time had passed and would never come back. For some reasons, the young child in me wanted to go back in time, before all the misery that went on, before the war. My inner child wanted to stay in that era, when she felt happy and young. The inner child in me had never grown, and yet was trapped inside an aging body and a wounded soul. I freed the child within myself after that last trip. The family I once knew as I'd known it didn't exist anymore.

Although that chapter was closed, the gate, which guided me to endless guilt trips remained open. I felt sad that I didn't spend any time with Mama and not enough time with Papa for the last years *of their lives. It felt as if the right of being around them had been viciously taken away from me. Destiny had stolen so many things that I could never replace.*

Was it all my fault? Theirs or Manoochhr's? Who could I blame it on? Perhaps no one; couldn't it be an ugly scenario written by Almighty God? I regret so many things that I've done. I carry so much guilt about so many things, who is to say who to blame? I wonder. Did Papa really ruin my life? Throughout the years, that question had hunted me in my head. In time, I couldn't even be sure; couldn't it just have been a play of destiny and nothing else? This is what I want to believe now anyway. But no matter what, it belonged to my past and I had to move on.

Pooya and I returned a few days after the funeral. I thought I did a good job at moving on, controlling my emotions and dealing with my loss. But a strange feeling had started to crawl inside me, a new fear. I started to have panic attacks very often. Pooya did his best to make me happy, but despite all his efforts I couldn't shake this new fear.

'What if I never see Sepideh? What if I miss the chance to see her ever again? What if I die and take that wish to my grave?' Disturbing thoughts of horror began to control me. I can't explain it. Before my parents' death, I kept thinking I could just go back, pick up all the pieces and start over. I always thought I would have time to be with my parents again. I would have time to see Sepideh again. That I would have time to put all the pieces back together again. But then, when I lost my parents, another fact of life hit me; people won't stay around for me to find time someday. Then I thought, 'What if I never get a chance to be a mother to Sepideh?'

"When she grows up she won't need me anymore, she wouldn't even know me. I will lose her forever." Finally, I expressed my thoughts to Pooya.

"She would always need you, Fariba," Pooya tried to reassure me. I looked at him and sighed.

"I hope you're right. I hope it won't be too late," I told him I know he saw the tears mounting at the corners of my eyes. He got up and walked toward me, sat next to me and held my hand.

"Fariba, I promised you that I would bring Sepideh back to you. I'll do that even if that is the last thing I do, I promise."

"Darling, it's not easy. How can you do that?"

"I made it back from the war; I got you out and free, didn't I?"

"Yes you did, and I'm thankful for all that for as long as I live."

"Then believe this. You and Sepideh will be reunited again soon."

I looked at his hazel eyes. They were sincere and promising, determined too. I kissed him and looked deep into his kind eyes.

"I believe," I told him.

"Well then, no more negative thoughts," he said and I remained quiet.

"Don't you want to sleep, my love? It's past midnight," he added as he got up.

"I lost track of time. I didn't realize it was that late."

I followed him into the bedroom, where I knew I would be safe once he held me in his arms.

~

*B*eing located on top of the hill made us somewhat secluded. The nearest house belonged to a middle-aged lady. I had seen her from time to time, just like I had seen some of the other neighbors. But as I told you earlier, I never socialized with any of them. I spoke to that middle-aged lady, for the first time when she came to borrow some salt.

"My name is Jihan, but I prefer to be called Saba," she said.

"Well, Miss Saba, I'm Fariba and I'm very pleased to meet you."

"Same here, but please don't call me 'Miss', just Saba," she requested.

"Why don't you come in?" I asked with a smile.

She stepped inside. She seemed very nice and in her late fifties, I thought.

"Oh my dear, you have a beautiful house. I love the colorings. It's dreamy—you know what I mean?"

"Yes, I know and I thank you. My husband and I did all the decorations and coloring ourselves."

"How nice; you know, my husband was a handy man, too. He used to do everything in the house, paint, repair and fix. God rest his soul; I miss him, though." Saba paused to float in the memories of her past. "But he's gone now," she added.

"I'm sorry, Saba, very sorry. I know how it is to lose a loved one."

"Isn't it sad? I mean since the war and all. It seems that everyone knows how it is to lose someone."

I felt a sudden gloom. What Saba said took me back to the war and all that went on then.

"Are you okay, dear? All of a sudden you became so pale," Saba asked.

"Yes, yes, I'm okay. It's just my mind, traveling back in time."

"Oh. Traveling back into the past, the era we all want to forget, don't we?"

"We sure do," I agreed.

"Look at me, I just came to borrow some salt and we started talking as if we've known each other for a long time." She laughed.

"Well, I'm glad that we had the opportunity to meet and talk," I said as I handed her a cup of salt.

"So do I. please say hello to your husband. You know, I met him before; it was when he just bought this house and was bringing some furniture in. He told me he was planning to get married and wanted to bring his bride here. He seemed like a very good man—good looking too—your husband. I hope you don't mind me saying that."

"No, not at all, I will tell him you said hello," I said with a smile.

"Thank you, darling, and have a nice day."

After Saba left, I couldn't help thinking how good it felt to be part of the world again. To have conversations with people, regular talk, ordinary stuff, neighborly visits and be able to socialize. I felt no longer a fugitive, but a regular housewife. It felt so good that it brought a smile on my lips that lasted for several seconds. More importantly, it brought peacefulness. Later, I told Pooya about my encounter with that neighbor.

"So, you met Saba," Pooya said. "She talks too much, but she's harmless; she's a nice lady."

"It felt good, Pooya, it was wonderful."

"Good, I'm very glad." He came forward and hugged me. I was truly free.

"Are you happy with me? I mean really happy?" Pooya asked "My! What a question! Am I happy with you? Darling, you are happiness itself, don't you know? I have you; I have happiness."

"I just needed to ask. I need reassurance from time to time, too, you know. But I'm glad that I asked. You always know what to say to melt my heart." He pulled me closer. His arms had a gentle, yet tight grip around me. "I don't know what I would do without you," he whispered softly into my ear.

"We have each other now and nothing can separate us," I told him. My head rested against his shoulder; shoulders that had been my head's resting place for so many years back. I looked at him deeply. Everything about him was the same, only he seemed more mature and wise. I noticed a few strands of gray on his temple.

"You made my hair white," he said teasingly.

"And you're a lot more handsome with it."

"Who? Me? Nooooo."

~

*A*s we lived our life together, we came across so many people. Some we liked, some we didn't. All that was part of life, of course, and every day that passed by I thanked God for every moment that I had with him, every experience, every bit of air we breathed in.

The only void in our perfect, happy life was the lack of Sepideh's presence, the only shadow that darkened my days. But I had hope, lots of it. Pooya gave it all to me; he brought hope back into my very existence. With hope I could do anything, I could reach the stars.

Our neighbor, Saba, became my very first friend in my new life after the escape. Despite our age difference, we were able to connect emotionally. I wasn't sure why I connected to her that well. Was it because for some reason she reminded me of Mama? I couldn't answer that honestly. Whatever it was, it filled the blank on those pages of my life when there was a need for a friendly female chat. I told Saba about Sepideh being away. Pooya didn't approve of it at first.

"I don't think you should tell her about Sepideh yet."

"She's harmless; you said it yourself, didn't you?"

"Yes I did. All I'm saying is to be careful when you want to talk about some details of your life, that's all."

I could understand his concern and of course I never mentioned anything about my life in prison or about the mental hospital. I just talked to her about Sepideh being away. It seemed that Saba could relate to me and my aching heart for my daughter. Later I learned why she understood my pain well.

"I had a daughter, too. She was only five when she died."

"Oh…I…I'm very sorry, Saba. I didn't know…otherwise I wouldn't have mentioned…" I stopped talking when I saw a teardrop at the corner of her eye.

"She had cancer; doctors couldn't do anything." Saba swallowed a big knot that was in her throat. "I watched my little girl die slowly and painfully. I watched her die."

Words ran away from my head. It seemed that I couldn't find anything to say to her; I just listened. I could feel her sorrow.

Finally, I was able to ask, "All these years, the time that passed by, it could never take away the pain, could it?"

"How could it? Time is just like an aspirin. It covers it up, it buries it deep inside, but it can never make it go away for real. It's just an illusion. You think you got over it and then from time to time, the pain comes back stronger than ever. It makes you feel it all over

again. It makes you realize that it was never gone, that you never got over it," she explained.

"Saba, I never thought of time as an aspirin, but now I can see what you mean. A pain that deep, it never goes away. I'm truly sorry for your loss, for what you went through."

"It was fate, I guess. Sometimes it helps when you blame everything on destiny, when you say God wanted it that way, although it seems so unfair."

"Did you ever try to have another child?" I asked.

"No..." She sighed. "I was too fearful. I was afraid that if I had another child, the same thing would happen again. I couldn't deal with it."

"What about your husband?"

"What about him?"

"Didn't he want to have another child?"

"He didn't take the death of our daughter any better than me. He suffered too much. He was heartbroken. When I told him about my fear, he said he understood and we never spoke about it again.

"That's very sad. I don't know what to say, Saba."

"You don't have to say anything. You listened to my story. You cared to hear me. That was wonderful, thanks."

Saba held my hand and I gave her a big hug. Her warm tears met my cold shoulder as my tears reached the corner of my lips. Thoughts kept running into my head. I thought about the game of life, the roles we play and how we play it. I thought how wonderful it would have been, if I could have another child myself. But unfortunately, a wishful thought was all it could be.

I didn't want to let those thoughts get out of hand; I had so much to be thankful for. I had a life to live. Lots of positive things had happened and I had no time for anything negative. Just like Pooya had told me: "no more negative thoughts."

Pooya and I were happy and we didn't need a new child. I knew someday Sepideh's laughter would brighten the room and make our world just perfectly complete.

For the time being, we had to be patient and be happy with what we had. Pooya had begun his work in a center he newly had opened for disadvantaged children. He took pride in what he did; providing medical care and other necessities for the poor gave him a sense of purpose. As for me, just when I thought I couldn't possibly love him more than I already did, each day passed and proved me wrong.

Chapter 9

*O*ne beautiful autumn day, around one o'clock in the afternoon, Pooya came home early.

"You're so early today, are you okay?" I asked.

"Yes I'm okay. We're going for a ride?"

"Ride?! Where are we going?"

"I'll explain to you once we reach there," he said.

He seemed to be excited about something. I could see it in him, but didn't question it anymore. I put on my veil and got ready.

After about two hours of driving, we reached Esfahan. It had been a couple of years since I had visited the city. I couldn't imagine in a million years that the city I once knew had changed so much. So mesmerized by the changes, I didn't realize we were almost at the center of the city until I noticed we passed Chahar-bagh Avenue. Finally, he turned left and stopped at the corner of a quiet street with tall oak trees on both sides. I couldn't remember which street we were on, but it looked familiar.

"Why did we stop here?" I asked naturally.

"Look there, you see that building over there?" He pointed at a large building in front of us.

"It's a school! So...?" I paused; I wanted to say, 'So what's the special thing about it?' But I swallowed the rest of my sentence. I stared at Pooya and then looked at the school. Pooya remained quiet. He knew I figured it out.

"It's Sepideh's school, isn't it?" I trembled. Pooya nodded. I gazed at the building. Then I looked at my watch, it showed three thirty. 'The school must be closed at this time,' I thought. Pooya had read my mind as usual.

"As you know, the school hours are usually eight o'clock to three o'clock. But they have special art classes on Wednesdays, sort of an after school program." He paused.

My eyes fixed on his eyes, waiting for him to continue.

"Some children attend this class...."

"And Sepideh is one of them." I finished his sentence. "Is she going to come out soon?" I asked anxiously. My eyes begged for a positive answer.

"Yes. She'll come out soon, in about fifteen minutes or so," he answered.

"Oh God, what am I supposed to do?" How could I possibly see my daughter after all those years and not jump out and run toward her? How do I not hug her and say, 'You're in my arms at last'? Crazy thoughts ran around inside my brain, one after another. I became very emotional. My knees, my arms, no, my whole body started to shake.

"You have to control yourself; otherwise, I won't show her to you," he demanded. He seemed very serious.

"Yes, I'll be whatever you want me to be. I...I'll be calm. I'll act in any way you want me to act...I promise." I had no idea how to keep my promise.

"Okay. In about fifteen minutes, more or less, she will come out of that brown door. A lady will be there to pick her up. She takes her to that car, the white Benz that is parked at the corner, right there. Do you see?"

My eyes followed the direction of his pointed finger and I saw a Benz I knew, Manoochehr's car. I jumped back on my seat, panic crawled under my skin. The thought of being that close to Manoochehr brought pure fright into my every cell. My heart began to race, Pooya held my hand.

"Calm down, Fariba, calm down."

"I can't help it. Do you see how I'm shaking?"

"Fariba, he can't hurt you now. He doesn't even know that you're here."

Despite what Pooya told me, I kept thinking that Manoochehr was looking at us. He knew we were there, I feared.

"He's staring at our car," I said with panic. Terror wrapped itself around me.

"No, darling, how can he know? It's only your imagination," he tried to reassure me.

On one hand, I wanted Pooya to just drive away. On the other hand, I had to see Sepideh. I think I wanted to say: 'Go, Pooya. Please go." But my inner voice yelled at me, 'No, take control, no fears. Be strong, wait and see her.'

I guess a mother's love can overcome any fear, because I didn't ask Pooya to drive away. I felt that my fear subsided and I became more relaxed. Pooya had a good point; how could Manoochehr see me in this car? 'How could he possibly know that I'm nearby? How could he ever recognize me with the veil covering most of my head?' I told myself.

Finally the door opened. A few children came out; I kept looking at each one with my hungry eyes. My eyes searched and tracked down every little face and tried to find familiar features. 'She must have changed a lot,' I thought.

Most of the children were out, but there was still no sign of my daughter. My heart pounded and I hoped to see her. My chest tightened every time an unfamiliar child came out. Impatient and nervous I wanted to run inside the school and find her. Suddenly the back door of the Benz opened and a woman, wearing a black chador, got out of the car. I knew her; Soltan looked almost the same. My eyes followed her as she went toward a child, standing alone by the brown door.

"Oh my God," I heard myself saying as I pressed my fingers on Pooya's hand. There, I saw my daughter, my beautiful, innocent Sepideh. She stood right there. I could see her so clearly. She had the same face I remembered. But she seemed taller and looked thinner.

Every little step she took toward Manoochehr's car, my head hammered forcefully. I didn't want her to get into that car. Only God knew how I felt; only God knew the storm inside my heart at that moment. My left hand kept its hold on Pooya's hand and it continued to tighten its grip even more. My right hand clenched the door's handle, ready to open it. Every cell in my body wanted to call her name. I wanted to get out of the car and run toward her. Tears of joy started to fall at full speed, running down my face and my chin, finding their way to my neck.

"My Sepideh. My sweet little Sepideh..." I kept saying.

All this happened so fast, there was not enough time to do anything. Sepideh got in and the car drove away and took me with it. My physical body remained with Pooya, but my heart and thoughts continued to follow their Benz long after my tearful eyes couldn't any more.

"Are you okay?" Pooya's voice brought me back to our car. I nodded.

"Then...may I have my hand back, please?" he asked with calm.

"Oh my God...Pooya, your hand!" I screamed. My nails had cut the skin on his palm and it bled.

"I'm sorry, I'm truly sorry. I didn't realize—"

"Its okay my darling, its okay. It must have been a twister in your heart."

How right he was; it had been a storm in my heart, which had already started to calm by the kindness in his voice, and by the compassion he offered. I must have kissed him a thousand times for being that patient, that kind, for being the angel that he always had been. He held me tight in his arms to ease my emotional pain. He held me for a while until I felt serene.

Then he said, "We're going back now. We have things to do."

"What things? What are you talking about?" I asked. I had no idea what he had in mind.

"I did some research on the school. They have a volunteer program and you, my dear, will be a new volunteer. You'll be working in that school."

"What…?"

"You heard me; you're going to be in that school every day."

"What kind of work? How? I know nothing about teaching!"

"My dear, they won't ask you to teach. They need extra help in the cafeteria and the library, in the playground, too." Pooya stopped talking and looked at me carefully. I didn't say a word. I remained quiet.

"The whole point is for you to be able to see her every day for now, until we find a way to bring her back permanently."

"How can we bring her back? You don't…don't mean kidnapping, do you?"

"No, silly…. My God! Kidnap her? Are you out of your mind?"

"I…I was just asking?"

"No, darling you don't want to have more problems with the law. No…no. We will find a way to solve this matter when the time comes. Meanwhile, I just want you to be able to see her and…."

I didn't listen anymore. I traveled into my own world again. See her every day? That's what he said and his words guided me to the land of my dreams, where I could picture myself playing, talking and holding hands with Sepideh. I can't tell you how I felt.

Like Pooya had told me earlier, we had work to do. Pooya wanted to prepare a good resumé for me. I had to work on a few things myself. I needed to learn to act normal. I needed to act calm, especially around Sepideh, no matter how anxious and excited. Questions started to fill my head up about the whole idea of me working there as a volunteer. Pooya knew me well enough to realize he had to explain things more clearly in order to shake off my anxiety.

"They would check you out, but they would find nothing that can exclude you from the volunteer program," he explained.

"Did you say they would check me out? What if they realize I went to prison?"

"Relax darling. You keep forgetting the fact that you have a new identity. There is no connection between your new name and your past." Pooya paused and then said, "I have made some letters of recommendation, too."

"How on Earth did you manage to do all that anyway?" I asked curiously.

"I never thought I would say this, but serving during the war has its own privileges, especially if one makes it back, like I did."

"What privileges?"

"Darling, it wouldn't be possible to do all this if I never received the money that our Islamic government offered me. I told you before, with money you can buy lots of things, new ID's, a new house, a new place in society, even respect."

I remembered when he told me about all of those once before back in Shafa. As a veteran and a prisoner of the war he sure had gained a lot and by that I don't only mean wealth, but places in society which had no room for him years before the War when he worked in a factory. To me, what he became the most was a hero and not just in name but in the true meaning of the word.

The résumé Pooya prepared showed an excellent history of volunteer services and a few letters of recommendation supported it all. The rest was up to me. I had to get ready for the biggest role of my life. With a lot at stake, I knew that once I entered that school as a volunteer, nothing but my performance would pull me through.

I told Saba about the volunteer work and she supported the idea of me working in that school as well, not because she knew the real reason why I wanted to do volunteer work, but because she believed sitting home, doing nothing wasn't a good thing for a young woman like me.

"I think it's a wonderful idea. You're young; don't stay home. I did that and I tell you, I regret it." Saba let out a big sigh and then continued, "By the time I realized that I had wasted my life and had done nothing positive, it was too late, and I wasn't young anymore."

Saba stopped to think for a second and then she added. "When you're old, nobody wants your services, even if you offer them for free. Isn't that sad?" She questioned, but didn't wait for an answer. "Listen, do what you can. Later in your life, when you look back, you'll be happy that you did something good."

She left after giving me credit for what I had planned to do, but I couldn't help thinking that I didn't deserve such credit. I had my own agenda behind the community service I wanted to do.

A few weeks later, after having mentally prepared myself, I went to the school for an interview. The principal, Mitra Kashani a middle age woman, very cold and formal, didn't ask many questions. To be honest, I took that as a sign of rejection. I thought that she didn't like me because she didn't seem very friendly.

I wasn't happy when I left the school. But still, I waited impatiently day after day, hoping for the phone to ring. Four weeks passed by and right when I started to think they would never call, the principal of the school called. She asked me if I was willing to start my volunteer work in the upcoming week. There is no need for me to tell you how I answered her, but I'll tell you anyway. "I'd be delighted," I told her.

I had one week to get ready for work. I can't tell you how endlessly Pooya tried to make me emotionally ready to see Sepideh up-close and personal and act normal at the same time.

~

*M*y work in the school started, and with that, the journey to motherhood began once more. At first, they put me in the cafeteria to help with children line ups, and then to make sure they were eating or sitting with their own groups. The first day seemed more of a challenge because I didn't know at what time Sepideh's class would be coming to the cafeteria and how I was going to react once I saw her. Everything seemed unknown. I finally found that out when I saw her. Sepideh and her classmates entered the lunchroom exactly at twelve thirty.*

My heart stopped for a few seconds when I first located her in the new group that entered the lunchroom. Then I remembered what Pooya had told me: "It is very essential and necessary for you to act normal." I think that day, that moment in the cafeteria I performed the best act of my life; being torn apart inside, I showed no special emotions on the outside. I wanted to hold her so tight, to shower her with my kisses, but I couldn't.

Sepideh seemed to be a very quiet little girl, almost too quiet. I helped her with her food tray; she didn't even look at me. I didn't think she would have recognized me anyhow, even if she did look.

I still don't know how I survived that day. Well, life is not easy; you know that, everyone knows that. But most of all, I know that. I realized that I had to suffer some more before I could actually hold her in my arms, look into her eyes and say: "Mommy is here." But God gave me the strength and, as each day passed, I found it a little easier to deal with my emotions around Sepideh.

I did read books to her entire class at the school library. I stood at the playground, watching her play on sunny days. I helped her with so many school projects. Very soon, I became a familiar face and she called me, "Miss Fari". Although I knew she wouldn't recognize me, I couldn't help feeling a little hurt when she didn't remember me as the mother she'd once had. I didn't blame her of course, how could she remember? Sepideh was very little when all that happened, when they erased me from her life. I thought about the days and the nights, when she might have needed me and I had not been there for her. She couldn't remember how I looked like anymore. Her memories of me must have been so vague by then; if she had any at all. The guilt inside me never left, never left me for one second.

My life became a lot more colorful with both Sepideh and Pooya back in it. I watched my daughter as she played with her classmates, as she ate her food, as she talked to her friends and as she read in the library. I tried to learn her facial expressions and body language. I learned quite new things about her. It was fun to know her all over again. I saw a little of myself in her. The shape of her face, she had my eyes, too. But believe me, it wasn't easy to do all that and at the same time be able to keep all my feelings hidden. It wasn't easy at all.

I did well; I remained fair to all the children. The kids liked me and I liked all of them, too. All of my efforts to care for the kids turned me into one of the most favorite volunteer workers at school.

Six months later, I became a very familiar face to everyone and by then, the staff often asked for my help rather than anyone else's. Even the principal, Miss Kashani who, "never commented on anyone's good work," as a teacher once said, was amazed how the kids liked me.

"We always had volunteers who came here to work and help. But you seem to have a passion for children. You really enjoy what you do." Miss Kashani said one day as I helped her with some paperwork in her office.

"Of course I enjoy what I do. These children are little angels," I answered her.

"Do you have children of your own?" she asked and somehow I found her question hard to answer, but I answered.

"Yes, I have a little girl. She is ten." I hoped that she wouldn't ask another question about my child, afraid that if she did I would break down and cry.

"She must be very lucky to have you as a mother. Someone..."

I wasn't so sure about her being lucky. My inner voice interrupted my thought to throw the question at me: 'Is Sepideh really lucky to have a mother like you?' Before I could answer the inner voice, Miss Kashani's voice pulled me back and got my attention again.

"...so caring," she said with a smile.

"I'm sorry, what...?"

"I said she must be so lucky to have you as a mother, someone who's so passionate and caring."

"Thank you very much. It's very kind of you to say that."

"But it's true. I see you; I see the joy in your eyes."

"Well, thank you. I'm grateful that you gave me this opportunity to work with kids."

"Did you ever pursue a career as a teacher?"

"No, I never did."

"*I think you should.*" *She paused to smile and then added,* "*You'd make a good one.*"

"*Well, perhaps one day,*" *I said and returned her smile with another as I started to arrange the papers, pretended to be focusing on the job at hand. I hoped that she would see me concentrating and would not ask any more questions. It worked; she left me alone and went to her own files.*

~

I felt blessed working in that school. I had learned so many new things about Sepideh. I noticed her taste in colors had changed as well as many other things. As I recalled, her favorite color used to be yellow, but I saw her choose light green as the best. She picked the 'Adventures of the Little Fish' as her preferred book, not 'Snow White' as she used to. I felt real pleasure to know her all over again. She showed so much interest in books. I remembered the past when she wanted me to read short little stories at bedtime. Now she wanted to read the stories herself. She wanted to be a story teller.

She seemed very smart and did well in her classes. Sometimes I asked her to show me her schoolwork and she took joy in showing me the grades her teacher gave her. I befriended her teacher, too, and asked questions that could indirectly give me some idea about how she did in her classes.

Sometimes, when Sepideh wasn't looking, I took one of her paintings or test papers from her school bag and brought it home, just to show it to Pooya. Almost every day, when I got home from school, I waited impatiently for him to arrive, so that I could talk about Sepideh and what had happened in school that day. He always listened to my stories very carefully and with excitement. Pooya looked at me with so much love in his eyes that it penetrated my heart deeper and deeper every day. He felt very happy for me and I, too, experienced joy like never before.

As time passed, my relationship with Miss Kashani, the principal, changed for the better. Ever since we had that little conversation in her office, I noticed an improvement in how we related. But after a while, I could see even bigger changes. She started to be very friendly. She took time to talk to me every time we met in the hallways. Very often, our conversations were about work and children.

I think I mentioned before, in the beginning, I judged her rather harshly. I remembered well my first impression of her was that I should keep my distance. But little by little, I realized how wrongly I'd misread her. Her cold way of speaking was not deeply rooted in her personality. She simply used that to mask her big heart. When it came down to personal lives, hers in particular, she remained silent. She needed to bury her soft heart under the rules and responsibilities of a principal and that's what she did. She acted firm and strict to the point where one could think she had no heart. But if one cared to look closer into her soul, one could see evidence of a caring person; especially if caught off guard and it wasn't easy to do so. She didn't like to engage herself in social gatherings because she didn't want people to see the softer side of her and lose respect. And of course, caging and limiting herself to work didn't leave her with anything but a deep loneliness.

I felt sad for her at times. Somehow, I could relate to her lonely world because I had lived it too, in the past. Unfortunately, there was nothing I could do to help her; she didn't seem interested in opening the doors to a more societal life. At least, that's how I believed it to be, but once again I judged wrong.

Her invitation for a mid-day tea break came as a shock. Surprised by her sudden change of behavior, I happily accepted. That first thirty minutes at the corner tea-room was the beginning of our friendship. Soon, our trips to the tea-room became routine and we talked about so many things, mostly school matters and then, one day she began to talk about herself. Puzzled at first, I didn't know why she opened up to me.

Thousands of different thoughts and possibilities rushed into my head at once. For a moment, I even thought she knew about my past and wanted me to open up by watching her doing so herself. I never gave a clue to anything that could lead to my past and I just continued to observe and listen. Soon I realized that all she needed was a friend and, for some reason, she judged me as one. Still surprised, I welcomed the new friendship.

Of course, when I told Pooya about my growing closeness with Miss Kashani, he made it clear to me that no matter how close she and I got, the fact that I was Sepideh's mother had to remain hidden. I totally agreed. I didn't want to sabotage my new connection with my daughter. I couldn't afford losing her again.

Mitra Kashani never had any kids. Her husband had left and divorced her after a doctor simply told him that his wife was barren. She wanted so much to be a mother and the fact that she couldn't, became a real tragedy and left her heartbroken. But when her marriage fell apart, she found herself abandoned and rejected as well.

Then the school became her whole life and she ran it like a man would. I knew the children were all scared of her, including Sepideh. I had seen how silence filled the room as she walked in. The children were not the only ones who disliked their principal; most teachers also felt the same, because they never saw the soft side of her. No one did and she made sure of that. I don't know why. But I did see beyond her mask and I think she realized it. That's why she started to think of me as a friend. For once, she could be herself and didn't have to hide behind the mask to be respected. For her employees, she remained the same; she kept a distance and kept her rules, which they had no choice but to obey. So many times, I wanted to tell Sepideh that she didn't have to be scared of Miss Kashani. But I didn't say anything to her. I respected Miss Kashani's ways and the image she preferred to project. It worked for her in running the school and she kept it under control.

❧

I felt real joy for the time I spent with Sepideh every day. Although, Pooya and I knew that we couldn't just settle for that. We still had a long way to go and a goal to reach.

"It'll be over when I bring Sepideh here, when she can physically live with us," Pooya said on a cold February day.

It snowed all day and the storm wasn't over yet. We were sitting at the dining table, having our dinner. The windows were all steamy. Unlike the weather, we were warm and calm.

"Pooya, I know that you're trying to find ways to make that happen and I know that you would never rest until it's done. I know you, and I'm blessed to have someone like you by my side." I told him as I pulled my chair closer to land a warm, loving kiss on his lips.

I had come a long way as far as healing, forgiving and moving on was concerned. But none of that would have been possible if it hadn't been for Pooya. He became the support system behind me. He became the rope that connected me to hope and held me together. In fact, he became everything I ever needed. I just had to look at him and I wanted to heal faster. I wanted to be the woman he fell in love with years back. I wanted him to see me the same way, as I was before. I thought about the day we met and how that had changed my life and how he had come through for me when no one else did or could. "My angel" I called him and he truly was an angel.

"I think I have said that a few times already, haven't I?" Grandma asked as she smiled.

"Yes, you have," I agreed.

You know, my darling, "life" is a strange thing. It can be so cruel and wrong one minute, and right the next. In our lifetime, we come across bad and good, evil people as well as angels. If we are lucky, we realize that angels may be around us, as ordinary people. They don't have to have feathers and be all shiny and white. They can just look like any man or woman we pass by in the streets every day. The same is true for evil and bad. Yes, my dear, we come across all kinds of people or forces and we better be ready for all that life has up its sleeve for us. That much I learned from life. I can never be too happy or too sad. Nothing is permanent.

*T*he spring ended and so did the school year, which only meant the beginning of the summer break. Just the thought of not being able to see Sepideh during that period crushed my heart. But I also knew that she needed some time off from school to just be a kid; to play and enjoy summer without worrying about classes and homework. I remembered how I used to feel at the end of each spring. Needless to say, all kids felt happy to be off from school for three months. Realizing that need, I dealt with my own feelings and wished her a happy summer. A week later, Manoochehr registered her for summer school. Selfishly, I felt happy at first, but then guilt kicked in and made me feel sad for her.

"I don't know why Manoochehr wants her to be in school all the time. She's a little girl and needs her summer vacation," I told Pooya with anger.

"Why are you so angry? At least you can see her the whole summer."

"At first, I thought how good that would be—if schools were not closed in summer and I could just see her all the time. But then, I thought how selfish it is to just think about my own feelings, my own needs." I paused and looked at Pooya to see if he wanted to say anything. Slightly leaning on the corner of the kitchen counter with his arms crossed, he just looked at me patiently.

"I'm listening, darling," he said.

"Well I just don't think it is fair for her to be in school all year round. He registered her in an after school program everyday and now summer school?"

"You may be right, but unfortunately, darling, we can't do anything about that. Right now, Manoochehr is the decision maker in her life."

"Maybe I can ask Miss Kashani to talk to Manoochehr."

"How are you going to ask her to do that?"

"I will think of some way."

"No, darling, I don't think that's wise, it may raise her curiosity about you and your true intentions."

"I know how to talk to her; we've been friends, remember?"

Pooya disagreed; but with my mind made up, I wanted to give it a try. So, the next day, I volunteered to help Mitra type some papers in her office. 'That should give me some quality time to talk to her,' I thought.

At her office and behind her desk, she did seem her usual self, so I dared and asked, "Mitra, I was looking at the list of the kids that are registered for summer school and I couldn't help but noticing that Sepideh…what's her last name again? Sepideh…Sepideh—"

"Which grade is she?" she interrupted without looking at me.

"She's in third grade, in Mrs. Farhang's class."

"Do you mean Sepideh Taban?" Busy with her files and still not looking at me she asked: "What about her?"

"Well…she doesn't need all these classes, don't you agree?"

She lifted her head up and stared right at me; she didn't say a word.

"I mean, she…she doesn't need all this schooling," I continued, although bothered by her stare. Thank God she took her eyes off of me and returned to her files.

"I agree," she replied. "But apparently, her father doesn't think it is too much." She looked at me from over the top of her glasses. "It is not good to get so emotional about these kids, you know."

"I'm not being emotional."

"You're starting to care more than you should. You can't be bothered by what these parents decide."

"Well, I…I just think it is wrong. Also, I've never seen her having a close friend. I mean, she's never had a friend over to her house and she's never gone to a friend's house."

"And how do you know that?" She stared at me again.

"Simple. One day at the library the kids and I were reading about activities with friends. Sepideh mentioned that she never had a friend over and never went to a friend's party."

"Lots of parents don't let their kids go anywhere or have activities outside of school. I see that all the time."

"Don't you think it is not—"

"Look, I can't run their households," Mitra interrupted me. "I can't tell them how to raise their kids. This is how things are in some families, whether you and I agree or not."

I remained quiet and she turned back to her files. I wasn't going to say anything else. It was no use; she wouldn't talk to Manoochehr even if I asked her to. I started to type. A few minutes passed and the silence in the room started to yell uncomfortably.

"You're very fond of that particular girl, aren't you?" she suddenly asked.

Although thankful for the shattered silence, I didn't really want her to ask me that.

What did she mean by that? Why did she ask if I am fond of her? I didn't want her to be curious about my feelings toward Sepideh.

"Well, why not?" I answered with calm. "She's a very sweet kid; why shouldn't I be fond of her?" I continued to type. I didn't even lift my head to look at her.

"Just for your sense of curiosity and between us, I'll tell you a little about her."

'Good,' I said to myself; she didn't suspect anything. All ears, I wanted to listen to what she knew about Sepideh.

Mitra got up and walked toward me. She sat on the chair next to me, took her glasses off and continued, "This little girl lives with her rich father and her stepmother. I believe that the stepmother makes her husband register the child for all these classes—after school, summer school and all."

"Why do you think so?"

"She doesn't want her around."

"Where is Sepideh's mother?" I asked calmly.

"We don't know exactly. Allegedly, she's in jail and mentally sick." She put her glasses back on as she got up again and went back to her desk.

"Oh." That was all I could say. I didn't make any comments and continued to type. My silence ended that particular conversation. My mind remained busy with all kinds of thoughts.

Later on, when I told Pooya about the discussion I had with Mitra, he seemed very displeased.

"You're putting your guard down by asking these questions," he complained.

"She didn't suspect anything. She just told me that I'm getting too attached to these kids." I defended my deed.

"I'm sure she realized that you're a bit more curious about Sepideh in particular."

"Well…she said…she said that I'm very fond of that girl."

"This isn't good, not good at all." I noticed a trace of anger in his voice.

"Pooya, darling, I kind of know this person by now. She's my friend and she's not a bad person."

"By the way you described her before, she sounds too strict to me. People like that don't like to bend the rules for anyone. If she finds out who you are, she will call the police and you'll be back in that hospital." Pooya seemed very worried.

"Pooya, calm down…calm down…please, darling." I spoke low and calm.

"Fariba, I worked hard to find you. I worked hard to get you out. I worked hard to get you a new identity so you could live again. Giving money to do all this was the easy part of it. But to do it right required lots of planning and time. To make it all happen, I had to plan every detail, every…"

He stopped. He walked toward the window and looked outside for a moment, as if he wanted to cool down. I remained quiet and waited for him to speak again. He turned around and took a deep breath.

"Look, we have come a long way only to go back to square one. I don't want to lose you, that's all." I saw tears in his eyes. I walked toward him and held both of his arms.

"You won't lose me, my love…Pooya, look at me…we're safe now. I have a feeling that God is watching over us now."

He looked straight into my eyes, a profound look. He didn't say anything.

"*I promise that I won't ask any more questions about Sepideh that will jeopardize our lives, or our future. But we have got to find a way to bring her back to us somehow.*" *I looked at him intensely as I talked.*

"*We will,*" *Pooya answered before he walked away. He took his jacket and went to the door.* "*We will, and that's my promise to you,*" *he added, before he stepped out and closed the door behind him.*

I have to confess, to see him like that worried me. He always remained calm and together, but not that day.

I could understand his fears and concerns. But I believed he judged Mitra wrong, too. He didn't know her, not the way I had come to know her. Somehow I knew, or should I say I felt, that she would never hurt me. But I had made a promise to Pooya that I wouldn't ask any more questions and I fully intended to keep my promise.

~

*V*ery soon, summer arrived and summer school began. Naturally, I asked Mitra to let me continue my work as a volunteer during the summer season and naturally, she agreed.

"*Are you kidding, I can always use your help around here,*" *she said with a smile.*

So I began my work again. Although, through the regular school year I had connected with Sepideh, but our real connection happened during the summer classes. I knew that she wasn't so happy about spending those hot summer days in school, so I tried my best to make those days a happy, pleasant experience. I helped her with her little projects and everything else, as much as my job allowed me to. The fact that only a small number of children attended the summer program made it a lot easier for me to pay extra attention to my little girl. I did all that without being too obvious.

At some point in my life, I had learned to be slick. I think my marriage to Manoochehr had a lot to do with it; after all, in my life with him I did learn how to put on a mask to conceal my tormented heart. In school, I showed a calm surface and never gave away what lay beneath. It sounds like I want to connect theses two experiences by similarities, but I don't. Just like in my marriage, I became nothing but a character in the school. However, there is a world of difference between the two situations. In the marriage, I disguised my hatred for Manoochehr; whereas in school, I played a role to veil my love for Sepideh.

~

*D*uring the summer, I bonded very well with my daughter. At the library, she sat next to me. She volunteered to show me all of her art work and she told her classmates that I was her favorite.

"Miss Fari is very nice. She can help you with your project, too. She always helps me. Isn't she the best?" I heard her say to Neda, her classmate.

"My sister always helps me with my projects," Neda answered.

"No one helps me at home," Sepideh commented.

"Don't you have a sister?" Neda asked.

"My sister is smaller than me. She can't help me!"

"What about your mom? My mom helps me, too, sometimes," Neda said.

"I don't have a real mom." Sepideh paused and sighed. "She's dead."

Neda didn't say anything, but she held Sepideh's hand.

"Hey, let's go to that swing," Sepideh said and they both ran toward the swing.

I can't say how I felt, hearing her talk like that about me. I felt my heart being crushed under the heavy weight of regret and sorrow. Oh, how I wanted to hug her and say, "I'm your mother and I love you so much." But of course I never said it. How could I?

How cruelly they had led her to believe that I didn't exist anymore. How perfectly they had erased me from her life. I wanted to scream, I wanted to beat myself up, for I'd brought it upon her. Because of my actions, she had to grow up thinking she didn't have a real mother anymore. She had to know sorrow and grief at an early age. I couldn't help but picture her in my head as a little child being told her mom had died. Knowing how attached she had been to me back then, it must have been such horrific news for her to handle.

'Oh dear God, dear God, what have I done to her? What have I done?' I kept asking myself.

I would have given anything if I could have just gone back in time and made everything right for her. What could I do at that point? There was nothing I could do to change the past for her and as for her future, I could only hope for the best without certainties.

My knees couldn't hold me, I needed to sit. Motionless and quiet, I sat on the bench like a statue. Sharp pain hammered both my temples. I couldn't stay; I had to go home. I left the school early that day.

~

*T*he summer ended and another school year began with only a two week gap between summer school and the first week of fall classes. I didn't see Sepideh during those two weeks and I felt lost. I knew she needed those weeks away from school. The poor little girl couldn't just be in school all the time, could she? I couldn't complain; I mean, I argued about her being in school too much, didn't I? So, with that thought, I eased my own pain of being away from her.

When the first day of school began, I couldn't fit into my own skin. I got up real early, got ready and went to school. In the gym, I helped kids line up, but I didn't see Sepideh. I remembered seeing her name on the list for class number 21. So, I checked her class but didn't find her there either. She didn't show up that day. In fact, she didn't attend school that week at all. You can imagine how I must have felt. I felt lost; I couldn't handle it. Where was she? The question spun around my head. Pooya called me a nervous wreck. By the time the week had finished, I felt truly edgy, panicky and tense.

"What do you think happened?" I asked Pooya nervously.

"I'm sure nothing has happened and she's okay. Maybe she went on a trip with her father and she'll be back this week."

Despite his effort to calm me down, I couldn't relax.

The second week also started without Sepideh in school. I wandered around like a lost gypsy in the wasteland. Pooya tried to find out some information, but this time, all he found out was a big nothing.

"What has happened? Why didn't Sepideh come to school?" Ready to cry, I asked Pooya again.

"I wish I knew the answer, my love. I wish I knew." I could see the puzzled look on his face, too.

Another two weeks had passed by and still no Sepideh. I couldn't function anymore. I wasn't myself. Pooya never gave up and kept trying to find out what had happened. He even drove me near Manoochehr's house every evening. We sat in the car, a block away from the house and watched the house. We watched the house for hours.

"There is no activity," he said.

"What do you mean?"

"The house is empty."

"What? No…what do you mean the house is empty. You said they were home and didn't go on a trip."

"The person I sent to check them out told me that they're home. But obviously, they are not there."

"So what does this mean? Where are they?"

"Darling, I'm just like you; I need to find that out."

Dying to know what had happened to my daughter, I wanted to yell and cry. The whole time on our way back home I didn't speak; neither of us did. We both were assessing the situation in our minds.

That day passed just like the others. I hardly wanted to continue my volunteer help at the school. Each day, I pushed myself to go and continue, just for the hope of seeing her there again. Every day at school, I glanced inside class 21, hoping she would be there asking me to read a story—wishful thinking. More and more I realized that she wasn't going to come back to that school. A few times I wanted to ask Mitra and be straightforward about it. My promise to Pooya prevented me from blurting things out, from asking the damn question, to see if she knew why my daughter wasn't in school. But how long could I wait and not know? I had no patience left. For how long could I just sit and hope?

Already, a month and a half had passed. It seemed like an eternity to me. Pooya wasn't himself, either. He watched my sorrow increase every evening. He saw how heartbroken I had become and that hurt him, too, of course. I knew he had done his best to find out where the family had gone, but this time he just couldn't come up with any answers.

Enough was enough. I had waited more than enough and I couldn't anymore; I had to ask the questions. For some strange reason, I had a feeling that Mitra knew something about Sepideh. I can't say why, I just had a feeling.

So, one morning, I went straight to her office, knocked on the door and opened it without waiting for her to answer.

"Mitra, I need to ask you something." I stepped inside her office.

"Yes dear, What is it?.... Are you okay?.... You don't look fine."
She took her glasses off and waited for my answer.

"No...I'm not okay. I'm worried."

"Please sit down dear...worried about what?" she asked as I sat.

"I'm worried about Sepideh Taban."

"Oh...that sweet child?... Well, unfortunately, she is not attending this school any longer."

"But why? What happened? Did she change schools? I mean why? Is she okay?"

"My God, slow down. So many questions! I must say you were always curious and worried about that child, more than any other; any particular reason?"

She looked at me, straight into my eyes, a strange and serious look. I didn't answer. She repeated her question in another form.

"Why is it that you have so much interest in her?" Her tone of voice sounded more serious, too. I knew I had to answer.

"I...I just want to know what has happened to her. You know that I'm very fond of her."

I tried to show no emotions; it wasn't working. I couldn't do a good job.

"First of all, nothing has happened to her. Let me say this before you faint. Second of all, this is not about you being fond of her. I may not be sharp and quick anymore, but I'm not stupid either."

This conversation wasn't going the way I wanted. Instead of me finding out things, she was.

"You should have seen and listened to yourself a minute ago, when you asked those questions. You were ready to cut my throat for an answer," Mitra said.

"Me?... Oh, please. It's nothing like that." *I started to laugh. I knew I had acted a little strange, but I couldn't help it.*

This time, she remained silent and just listened to my fake laughs. So I added, "I mean…c'mon…look, I got worried when I didn't see her at school, that's all." *I smiled..* "Is that strange, to ask what happened to her?"

"Her teacher asked me, too, so did her gym teacher as well as the art teacher from the after school program. But none of them sounded like you."

"It's really nothing. I mean…isn't it a little odd? She attended the after school program, she attended summer school and then all of a sudden, she disappeared. So I got worried."

Mitra leaned back in her comfortable chair, put her glasses back on, thought for a few seconds and then said, "Well I suppose you're right. It does seem a little odd. I mean to see her in school all the time and then not to see her at all, not knowing why. I kind of understand." *She paused and I stayed quiet.*

"But she's okay. The family notified me of her not coming here anymore," *she added as she started to put organized papers into the folders to be filed.*

"When did they notify you?"

She looked at me in a strange way again. Did I have to ask? I tried to fix it again.

"I mean…why? I mean, she is such a sweet girl; I'll miss her."

I tried not to look into her eyes; I thought she would see the tears in mine. She didn't say anything; the silence in the room became a killer. I needed to leave; I got up.

"Well, I feel much better, thanks....oh...let me take these folders back to the file room." I grabbed some folders from her desk. As I turned toward the door, before taking another step, I heard her voice.

"Her father is dying," she suddenly said. An electric shock hit my body. The folders in my hand dropped to the floor. 'Manoochehr is dying?' my inner voice asked.

"What? Who?" I asked as I picked up the folders from the floor.

"Mr. Taban, Sepideh's father is sick. He has cancer," she explained. I couldn't talk. I waited to hear more.

"They called me on the phone. Apparently, he got worse and they decided to move to Tehran. There is a physician over there...my God! Do you want to sit down? You look pale."

I sat; otherwise I would have dropped to the floor myself. 'Manoochehr...dying? Did I hear it right?' some voice inside me asked.

"For how long has he been sick?" I asked.

"I don't know. I didn't ask. The wife said it took a sudden turn for the worse and there is no hope. But they still want to transfer him to a hospital in Tehran where that special physician works. Are you sure you're okay? Because you—"

"Did they say which hospital?" I cut her off. "Or where they will be in Tehran?"

Mitra looked at me deeply as she leaned closer on her desk, toward me. "You know...I can swear to God that you have some kind of personal agenda behind all this curiosity and questioning."

"Well of course I..."

"And please don't tell me it's because you just miss this student. This is beyond a volunteer/student relationship."

"I don't know what you mean...I'm going to the file room." I got up again, I felt weak. I wanted to sit back down, but I knew it was best not to.

"*Do you want to know where they live in Tehran?*" Surprisingly, Mitra offered! I turned to her and used all my strength to sound careless and calm.

"*It would be nice to know. I can send them some get well cards or something.*"

"*I wanted to send a card myself, on behalf of the school,*" she said.

"*So what's their address? I can send a card on your behalf, too,*" I told her.

"*I don't know if I should tell you…I don't have their permission to give their address away.*"

"*But, you…you just asked me if I wanted to know?*" She didn't answer. Annoyed and upset, I continued, "*You asked me if I wanted to know their address, didn't you? But now that I've said yes, you don't want to give it! What is this, Mitra, a game?*"

"*I know. I'm sorry, Fariba. I shouldn't have said anything. I already have told you too much. I'm not being professional at all.*"

She returned to her papers. She looked cool and calm. I, on the other hand, felt furious. With my blood boiling, I wanted to just drop the act, strangle her and take the words out of her. I began to breathe fast. I tried to be calm, but I couldn't even act calm. One…two…. three…four…I counted to give myself time to cool off and to come up with another solution. But cooling off wasn't possible. I felt like water in the boiler, already boiled and ready to whistle, so I did.

"*Tell me, Mitra, Tell me where Sepideh is!*" I took a few steps forward, toward her desk. The palm of my right hand landed hard on her desk as I demanded an answer.

Mitra looked shocked as she stared at my quivering body. She continued to stare at me as if I was a lunatic. For a moment, I didn't know what she wanted to do; call the security guard to throw me out? There wasn't any way out of this situation. It was too late to back away; the damage had been done. It was too late to fix it.

"*If you only knew…if you only knew.*" I started to cry.

"*Calm down…tell me. What's going on with you? Why do you want to know all these things about her?*"

"Because...because I am Sepideh's mother?!" I said it. No more games, no more play-acting.

"I'm her real mother," I repeated. Tears started to pour down, washing my face, leaving a salty taste at the corners of my lips. She got up and walked very fast toward the office door to close it. I didn't even remember leaving it opened as I came in.

"What are you saying, Fariba?" She stood between the desk and me. "All along, you were Sepideh's mother! The mother who was in jail? The mentally sick mother? The one who escaped from that mental institute I heard about? All along, you kept the truth from me!" She walked back behind the desk. "I can't believe my own ears."

She sat in the chair. She seemed very upset. I could see the rage in every line of her face. I didn't know whether she felt angry or more shocked than anything else, perhaps a little of both! At that point, did I care?

A few minutes passed without any of us say a single word. Finally she broke the silence.

"I can just call the police and tell them who you are and what you did." I lifted my head up and looked at her, but I remained quiet.

"But I won't...I don't like what you did, lying to me and all."

"What did you expect me to do? If I had told you the truth, if I had told you that I did time in jail and escaped from a mental hospital, would I still have had a chance to work here as a volunteer? If you knew all of that, then you wouldn't have let me work here."

"You lied to me; that wouldn't put you in a "trustworthy" category right now, would it?"

"Why don't you understand? I didn't have any other choice. I was a desperate mother who was trying to get close to her child."

"Mr. Taban had told me that you were unstable and your hospitalization was for your own good."

"Please, Mitra, look at me. We have worked together for the past year. You've watched me work with these kids. Did I ever give you any reason to believe that I was unstable?"

"I can't say you did. In fact, I'm very pleased with your work. I've said so many times."

"He put me there; he kept me there, but he was the one who needed to be locked up for his abusive ways. Look, I can't tell you my life's story right now. Please, I beg of you as one woman to another, tell me where my daughter is."

Mitra remained quiet.

"Sepideh is my little girl. She needs me; she needs me more than ever. If her father dies, she will just perish in the hands of her stepmother."

Mitra kept on listening and I kept on talking.

"Think about it, Mitra…she's better off with me, than with her. That woman doesn't even care about her. Do this for Sepideh, not for me, not for anything else, but for her sake…please."

I stopped. I didn't know what else to tell her. She got up and walked toward the wet, steamy window. I didn't notice until then that it had rained. She stared out into the street. I watched her.

After a long unbearable silence she spoke. "I will do this for Sepideh." As she said that, she walked to her desk and pulled out a notebook. She wrote something on a piece of paper and handed it to me.

219 Miran Avenue Niavaran, Tehran 81336.

I did read it a few times, as if I wanted to carve it on my heart.

"Thank you, Mitra, thank you so much."

"He's been going to Arvand hospital." She gave the last piece of information she had.

I hugged her. "I can't thank you enough," I said.

"There is no need for that. I did what I believe is good for Sepideh. If you are the person who I have come to know over the past year, Sepideh will be in good hands. Good luck." I felt very emotional and couldn't speak.

She then continued, "Go find her…go."

I left her office and the school altogether. I had to run home to tell Pooya we were going to Tehran.

Chapter 10

*B*eing only six hours away by car, we decided to drive to Tehran that same night. On our way there, thoughts and feelings kept crawling into my head, and into my heart. I had mixed emotions— fear, anxiety, excitement and joy all at the same time.

Only a little past sunrise, we reached the capital. We checked into Niavarana Hotel near Miran Avenue. Pooya made a few phone calls to Arvand Hospital. We found out Manoochehr had been hospitalized for only two weeks and then discharged. One of the nurses was kind enough to say there was nothing more they could do for Manoochehr.

"So, he's home. They basically sent him home to die," I said. I felt a sad sensation deep inside me. Did I feel sympathy? If yes, it certainly took me by surprise, I never knew I had sympathy for him; whatever it might have been, it was short-lived. Anger replaced it, with a trace of fear.

"So how do we get Sepideh out?" I asked. Pooya didn't answer. It seemed as if he wanted to think for a few minutes. "He's on his death bed. I don't think he has any strength to fight with me." I added.

"Oh, I'm not worried about him. I am worried about his wife's reaction. I don't want her to call the police," he said.

"She won't."

"How do you know that?"

"I don't know. I just have a feeling that she wouldn't do that."

"What if your feelings aren't right?"

"Pooya, let's just go in and talk to them. I'm sure she would be happy to get rid of Sepideh."

"I don't know about this. I say, let us do some thinking first. Maybe it's better if we wait until he's dead. It'll be easier to deal with her then."

"Pooya, you have changed!"

"Changed? What do you mean, in what way?"

"You used to do things with more ease. You're more cautious these days."

"You're wrong. I have always been cautious. I do things with full observation. I just don't do things without thinking. I don't want to risk anything. I don't want to lose you, Fariba."

"You're the sweetest man that has ever lived on Earth, do you know that?" I gave him a big hug.

"I know that," he said jokingly. "But how do you know I'm the sweetest man on Earth? How many men did you know before me?" He had a teasing smile.

"I just know. There just can't be any man who's sweeter than you. No way; it's not possible."

"Oh well, in that case, I thank you. You're sweet, too."

"Then we were made for each other," I said with a smile, "Yes indeed." He held me tight. "Everything is going to be okay. Very soon we will have Sepideh with us."

"You really think so, huh?" I asked.

"Yes, I do."

That night in our hotel room, as I rested my tired body on the bed, I contemplated about our little happy family—Pooya, Sepideh and I—being together. I fell asleep with that beautiful thought dancing in my head.

The next day, we drove to the house. We parked the car a few houses away.

"I just want to go inside and tell that man that I'm taking Sepideh with me," I told Pooya.

"I still don't believe that's a good idea," Pooya said as we monitored the house.

"Okay. So what do you think we should do?"

"I haven't come up with anything yet."

I kept quiet. We sat there in the car for two hours that seemed like an eternity. No one came in, nor went out. Around two in the afternoon, a taxi stopped in front of the house. I knew the man who got out of the cab and rang the bell. He looked exactly the same as I remembered him.

"Who's that?" Pooya asked.

"Manoochehr's older brother."

"Does he have other siblings?" he asked again.

"No." I paused and then said, "Pooya, I want to go inside."

"I don't think—"

"Please, let me go. I have a feeling that everything will be okay."

He thought for a few seconds then said, "Alright—let's go in. I'll go with you."

"No, please. I need to do this alone. I need you to stay in the car in case we have to drive away fast."

"I'm not going to let you go inside that house by yourself."

"Pooya, please—"

"Out of the question; you go, I'll go."

"Listen to me, darling, if he sees you with me, he may get angrier. After all, I'm still married to him if I go by my other name, remember?"

"It's too dangerous."

"Pooya, I need to go. I need to talk to him. He's dying. Who knows—he may come to his senses."

Pooya had a very serious face on. He didn't seem to be happy with my plan. Meanwhile, he didn't have a plan of his own. He put his head back on the headrest of the seat, closed his eyes and said nothing. I didn't say a word; I wanted to analyze the situation.

"Everything is happening so fast. We didn't have time to plan and you're very impatient. I don't like it, but I have no clue as far as telling you what to do. So...I say okay. I'm going to let you go in and I'm going to wait for you in the car right in front of the house. After fifteen minutes if you're not out, I will come in."

"I'll need more time to talk to him. Because..." I had to stop talking. The expression on Pooya's face gave a clear message, he was ready to change his mind altogether. "Alright...alright...we do that then. Fifteen minutes," I agreed.

"I still don't know why I'm letting you do this, but you've won. It's two o'clock now; by two fifteen, I'm going to come inside."

I kissed him and got out of the car. I stood still for a few seconds before making any other step forward. Weakened by fear, I started to walk. Finally, I reached the house and rang the bell. Someone buzzed me in without even asking who it was. I went inside, past a little garden and then arrived at another doorstep, I knocked.

"Come in; it's open," a familiar voice said. I knew that voice; it belonged to Zohreh, Manoochehr's wife. I went in, stood and looked around; a faint light came out of the slightly open door of a room on my left. I could see the corner of a bed. The room's door opened wide and Zohreh stepped out, followed by Manoochehr's brother. Except for having put on some weight, Zohreh hadn't changed much.

"May I help you?" His brother asked. He looked puzzled. He couldn't see my face since I had a black lace veil on. I went two steps toward them both.

"We're expecting some people. Are you the nurse we've—?" Zohreh asked right before my answer interrupted her.

"I'm Fariba. I'm Sepideh's mother." I removed my veil. None of them spoke, but I saw the shock all over them.

"I'm Fariba," I repeated louder. If still alive, I wanted Manoochehr to hear me from the other room, I could see him lying on the bed, but he wasn't moving.

"What is this woman doing here at my house?" his wife asked.

"*How dare you show your face here?*" *his brother said angrily.* "*Leave at once.*"

"*No, let me talk to Manoochehr. I came to see him.*"

"*Are you out of your mind, you crazy woman?*" *Zohreh said.*

"*Get out,*" *his brother ordered again and with that sentence he moved toward me, stretched his arm and showed me the door with his finger pointing at it.*

"*I'm not leaving unless I talk to Manoochehr.*"

"*How dare you come here and show your face? Have you forgotten what you did? You're a fugitive. I will call the Police right now,*" *Zohreh said.* "*Throw her out, please,*" *she demanded.*

"*As you see you're not welcomed here. My brother is dying and you think that I will let you upset him on his death bed?*"

He raised his voice and as a result of his yelling, Zohreh's kids ran downstairs to see what all the noises were about; among them was Sepideh. When I saw her running down the stairs, my heart melted.

"*Miss Fari?*" *Her eyes widened, for she didn't know why I stood there and why her uncle yelled. Manoochehr's brother took two large steps toward me, grabbed my arm and pushed me toward the door.*

"*You leave right now, or I will call the police.*"

"*Then you should call the police. I'm not leaving unless I talk to Manoochehr.*"

I started to fight him as he kept pushing me. He became very violent; he grabbed me by my shoulders and threw me against the door. I almost tripped and lost balance, but I got a grip on myself and stood straight.

"*I'm not leaving…I'm not leaving. Manoochehr…Manoochehr,*" *I screamed his name.*

"*You nasty woman; he doesn't want to see you. I'm going to call the police,*" *his wife said as she ran to the phone.*

"*Put down the phone. Let her come in. I want to talk to her.*" *I heard Manoochehr. His voice sounded so different than what it used to be. It sounded less harsh.*

His brother stopped fighting with me; his wife ran inside the bedroom to warn him.

"Manoochehr, you don't want to see her. She is bad news; you know that."

"I want to talk to her I tell you. Take the kids upstairs," he ordered his wife and then to his brother, "Let her in, brother."

Zohreh gathered her kids and called Sepideh to follow her upstairs. I will never forget the way she looked at me when she passed by. I waited until Zohreh reached the stairway before I moved toward Manoochehr's room.

"If you do or say anything to make him upset, I will kill you right here," his brother whispered in my ear. I just looked at him and didn't say a word. I entered the room. I could see Manoochehr closely and I couldn't believe my eyes. The way he looked, shocked me. The man lying there looked extremely thin and worn out. The cancer had taken its toll and had turned Manoochehr into a weak harmless creature I didn't know. I stood only an inch away from his bed.

"Sit down, Fariba." I sat. I could see the face of death. I almost felt sorry for him.

"I came to talk about Sepideh," I said with calm.

"I know," he answered.

"You know?"

"Why else would you put yourself in danger by coming here?"

"I'm sorry for what is happening to you—"

"Stop, Fariba, please don't. I know you hate me."

"I don't hate you, Manoochehr." As I said that, in my head I searched for the truthfulness of what I had just said to him. Did I hate him? Did I not? Maybe I did. I think I did hate him; except, for that very moment, I felt no hatred toward him.

"No...Manoochehr...I—"

The doorbell stopped me from finishing my sentence. I looked at my watch; exactly fifteen minutes since I entered the house. 'Oh God, it must be Pooya,' I thought.

"Open the door. It's Fariba's husband," Manoochehr told his brother. I looked at him, shocked by what I just heard him say.

How did he know that? I continued to look at him deeply with that question in my head. He stared right back at me.

"How do you know it's him?" I asked. "How much do you know about him?" I asked again.

He smiled a brief smile, shortened by a few heavy coughs.

A few minutes later, Pooya came in. "Are you okay, Fariba?" He started to walk toward the bedroom. Manoochehr's brother came forward to stop him from going in, but Pooya pushed him away and walked right inside.

"So, finally we meet face to face," Manoochehr said.

Pooya didn't answer, but came closer to stand beside me.

"Are you okay?" he asked again.

"Yes, I'm okay."

"Manoochehr, how did you know? How do you know him?" I asked again.

"It's not only this young fellow who pays money and hires people to find things out for him. I do the same."

"How long have you known about Pooya and me?"

"When they told me that you escaped, I hired a very good detective to find you and he did. I don't know how, but he did."

"And you never told the police?" I asked in disbelief.

"No, something had changed in me. I changed. I can't explain. I wanted to leave you alone."

He coughed again. I gave him the cup of water that was on the table next to his bed. After he drank the water, he gave the cup to me and I put it back on the table. His wife grabbed the cup and filled it up with water again. I noticed her standing there listening, after she had rushed back downstairs.

"I knew you worked as a volunteer at Sepideh's school. I had no problem with it. I just watched your moves from afar to make sure you wouldn't kidnap her."

"Manoochehr...you mean...all along you knew?"

"Yes. I think it's too late to say that I'm sorry for everything. I can't change the past..." The coughs started heavily and stopped him from talking. Zohreh offered a glass of water, but he didn't want it.

Pooya put his hands on my shoulders. I couldn't speak. I wanted to cry. Yes…I remember very well…I did cry.

"I know you're here to take Sepideh with you." Manoochehr had time to say in between the coughs.

"Manoochehr, I'm sorry for what is happening to you," I told him and this time I didn't have to search inside my head for the truth, I knew I meant it.

"Don't be sorry, because if it wasn't for the fact that I'm dying, we wouldn't be able to talk to each other in this manner." A faint smile sat on his lips. I couldn't help it, I kept crying.

"Don't cry, Fariba," Pooya said softly.

"He is right," Manoochehr said. "Don't cry. I want to tell you that I'm glad you came for her. I have been waiting to see when you were going to do that."

"But—but why didn't you tell me this before?"

"I don't know why? Who knows? Maybe I was sure that you would come to find her, to get her. I told my wife to give all the information to the school. I knew you were going to dig it all out somehow."

"Wait a minute, why do you want her to take Sepideh?" Zohreh objected to the whole idea of me taking Sepideh. "I've raised her since she was four years old. I'm going to take care of her," Zohreh argued.

"Be quiet. You just take care of your own children. The only reason you took care of Sepideh was because you were afraid of me. But after I'm gone, God knows what you would do to her."

"This is what I get after all I have done, being a good stepmother and all? I even—"

"That's enough, I told you to be quiet," Manoochehr interrupted her.

"Are you sure that you want her to take Sepideh?" his brother asked and then he offered to take Sepideh. "I can take good care of her, you know that."

"No brother, thanks. With me gone, Sepideh is better off with her own mother."

"But she's crazy," Manoochehr's brother protested. "How can she be—"

"Hey—watch what you say." Pooya rushed in, and didn't let him finish.

"We can ask Sepideh to come downstairs. She knows I'm sick and may die, although she never asked and I never told her. But she's old enough to know when things aren't right."

I felt very emotional. One may ask, why all the emotions? Why did I care about what had happened to him? I wish I could answer that, but I can't. Why did I care about the person who made my life a hell, made me suffer for so many years, away from my daughter? The person whom I hated, who had been the source of most of my nightmares? All those years, so many days and countless nights, I wished him dead. The time had come and his days on Earth were numbered and all I wanted to do was cry. Why wasn't I filled with joy? Surely my grief and sympathy for Manoochehr surprised Pooya, too—sympathy and grief? Did I really feel those emotions? I'm not so sure now, but back then, right at that moment, I remember how melancholy crawled into every corner of my heart.

"Okay, now you can take her with you." Manoochehr's voice brought me back inside the room from the depths of my thoughts. I turned and saw Sepideh standing by the bedroom door. She looked at her dad, then turned and looked back at me.

"Sepideh, there is something you should know. Come and sit next to me," Manoochehr said.

She went and sat on the corner of her dad's bed. She stared at him, waiting for him to speak. I looked at her and realized for the first time how mature she looked. It seemed as if she'd grown up over night.

"Darling, this is your real mother," Manoochehr blurted without any hesitation.

She turned around and looked at me. "No, Papa, this is Miss Fari; she helps us in school."

"I know Sepideh, but she also is your mother."

"No, my mother is dead, even mommy Zohreh told me so."

"*Sepideh, your mother isn't dead. Mommy Zohreh and I were mistaken. We made a terrible mistake and we are truly sorry.*"

I can't explain the way my daughter looked at me at that moment. In her face, I could see joy as well as pain. In her, I could see happiness and belief, but also sorrow and distrust. I knew she felt betrayed by me, and by everyone else she called family. At the same time, the thought of having her mother meant protection and safeguard. I could easily read all those emotions in her, although she remained quiet. I think she didn't know what to say. Perhaps, she wanted to be left alone for a while until she could adapt to all the changes coming her way.

"*Listen, Sepideh, you're going to go with your mother. You're going to live with her from now on. She loves you,*" *Manoochehr told her.*

"*What about you? Where are you going to be?*"

"*I have to go somewhere else. Some place far away.*"

"*I know where that place is…*" *Sepideh paused. With her head down, she stared at the bed linens, then added without looking at her dad,* "*You're dying, aren't you, Papa?*" *she asked straight forward.*

"*Yes, darling, I am.*" *He paused for a moment and then said,* "*I'm very sick. I've been sick for a while. You knew that, didn't you?*"

She lifted her head and looked deeply into Mannochehr's eyes. "*Yes, Papa, only I wasn't sure.*" *She sighed.*

Manoochehr said no word; no one did. Sepideh bent over and hugged him tight. She started to cry.

"*Papa, I don't want you to die,*" *she pleaded.*

Manoochehr's face became wet from the footprints of his own tears. For the first time I saw him cry. He didn't answer. I don't think he could speak; he must have had a big knot in his throat. He tried to hug her, only he couldn't, too weak to raise both his arms.

"*Go now, I need to sleep,*" *Manoochehr told her, but Sepideh didn't move.*

"*My brother will make sure that everything is taken care of. He'll send her things to you, Fariba. I also want Soltan to be with Sepideh,*" *Manoochehr said.*

"Where is she?" I asked.

"She's still in Esfahan, in our house."

"Wait a minute!" Zohreh jumped in. "What do you mean Soltan should go with Sepideh? I need her in our house. My kids need her."

"You and the kids don't need Soltan as Sepideh needs her. Soltan took good care of Sepideh, more than you ever did," Manoochehr told Zohreh.

"How can you say that? I cared for your daughter, when her own mother failed to be there for her."

"Stop talking, Zohreh. You think I never noticed the way you treated my daughter? You were never a good stepmother to her. Soltan and Sepideh are very attached to each other and Fariba got along with Soltan real fine back then when…" A series of coughs stopped Manoochehr from talking.

"Please go," Manoochehr managed to say in between the coughs. "I need time with my brother now. I need to arrange things."

I got up and held Sepideh's hand. She surrendered herself to me; I brought her to my arms. She cried silently, I held her tight and Pooya held me.

"Take care of my daughter, please," Manoochehr told Pooya.

"You know that we will," Pooya answered.

"Yes, I know." Manoochehr stretched out his arm in a hand shake posture. His skinny, unsteady arms had no strength. Pooya shook his hand and followed Sepideh and I out of the bedroom. As we left the house, rain started to fall. We drove to the hotel, packed and drove right back to Esfahan.

On our way back, when the rain was at its peak, Sepideh asked as she sobbed, "Is Papa going to be in heaven when he dies? Can I pray for him?"

"Yes, sweetheart, you can pray and yes, he'll be in heaven," I answered.

I prayed for him, too. I felt the heavy weight of sorrow on my chest and one of those knots sat painfully in my throat. Manoochehr was dying and I felt very sad. I thought how strange life had been.

Up until that morning, I had wished for his death every day. I held him responsible for all the misery, for all those years that I had suffered. But now that I saw him in his deathbed and saw how he had changed, my hatred for him unbelievably vanished and gave place to sadness, regret and grief instead. Why sadness? Why regret? You may ask.

I felt sad because I realized I didn't want him to die after all, and I regretted the fact that I wished him dead all those times. I grieved for someone who had been nothing but an enemy to me for years. For the first time, I also realized that Sepideh loved him. He was the only father she knew and he had been all she had for years. For some reason, I always thought Sepideh hated him just as I did, silly, isn't it? I knew I had to work hard to make the transition easy for her.

Manoochehr passed away a few days later and was buried next to Mom Taban, who had died a few years earlier. Most of his properties went to Sepideh, as his lawyer wrote in a letter. As Manoochehr requested, his brother did send all Sepideh's personal belongings and Soltan came to live with us a week after Manoochehr's death. His death closed another chapter of my life forever.

In the beginning, Sepideh kept to herself. She was very quiet; in fact too quiet and naturally, her silence worried me to death. But Soltan helped me realize that she still mourned the loss of her father. She grieved, not so much in words, but in silence and solitude.

At first, I wasn't sure whether or not she would accept me as her mother. But soon I understood she had no problem accepting me. In fact, she had always dreamed to have her very own mother back one day. The vague images of the mom she knew in her heart had never left her in all those years. She might not have remembered so much the physical aspect of her, but Sepideh had remained connected to those unclear memories of a caring mom she once had. Although, it took a while before Sepideh got used to the idea of calling me "mom". I remained as Miss Fari for the first few months of her living with us. I didn't have a problem with that either; because Miss Fari happened to be someone she had liked a great deal. I knew, some day she would crown me with my rightful title.

I must say, I waited impatiently for that moment to arrive; it arrived one day, when she called me mommy out of the blue and I just couldn't stop myself from jumping for joy. I hugged her as hard as I could.

I thanked God for having Soltan around. She made the transition a lot easier for Sepideh and helped her to accept the changes better. Soltan took care of her with so much love in her heart. In fact, she became a mother to us all, and also a best friend to Saba, our neighbor. They did connect very well and Soltan seemed very content to have found a friend.

My life with Sepideh and Pooya became something I would like to call "a dream"; my dream come true. Pooya proved to be a wonderful father to her and Sepideh loved and respected him, too. Although she never called him "dad", he was "Uncle Pooya" to her. To Pooya, she became the daughter I could never give him. The fact that I couldn't give him a child of his own still bothered me from time to time; even though he never gave me any reason to be concerned about it. In fact, he kept reassuring me that he had everything he wanted and that he couldn't wish for anything more.

"I have you, I have Sepideh and I am alive. What more can I ask for?" he always said. I knew he meant every word of it, too.

Pooya added two large rooms on top of the house: one for us and one for Sepideh. Soltan took over our old bedroom downstairs. We bought new furniture and painted the whole house again. We painted Sepideh's room in a very light pink and she picked white curtains for the window. She had white shelves for stuffed animals and books she liked to read, a white dresser and a round light pink rug. For our new bedroom walls, we chose the lightest green, which went well with our white window treatment and a darker green rug. A tall, widespread and exotic foliage right above our bed looked striking and I loved it.

Soltan decorated her room in colors and styles she wanted. She said she had always dreamed of having a room with gold and light brown colors and that's what she got. Everybody seemed to be happy and everything looked new—a fresh start, a new chapter.

Years passed by quickly. At twelve years old, Sepideh seemed relaxed and she was becoming. I couldn't believe how much of me I could see in her. Physically, she looked so much like me. It felt very good looking at her and having her close. We all experienced life as a whole family together and it felt great. I could finally see life as a wonderful thing, as complete and as a miracle. Living meant joy and happiness. Alas, little did I know that happiness wasn't going to last forever.

For a good while, I lived my life under the sun and had forgotten how a cloud could darken a sunny day, and how a frightening shadow could chase happiness away. I forgot that life wasn't, and never remained a fair game for a long period of time—not for me anyway.

In spring, Pooya's sister Shiva came back to Iran from England for a short visit. I can't explain how happy and excited I felt seeing her again. I couldn't remember the last time Shiva and I had talked face to face.

She hadn't changed much, more mature perhaps, but still as sweet as I remembered. She looked beautiful in her blue Islamic outfit. Her flawless, peaceful face showed no trace of hardship. Her marriage was a success and she had two wonderful boys: Nima was four and Nader only two. She and her two children spent almost a month with us, a time to remember.

However, Shiva had to return back to England and in order to do so, she had no choice but to travel from Esfahan to Tehran's international airport. At first, she decided to take a plane and fly to Tehran, but later she changed her mind.

"I forgot. I have to see Aunt Kobra," Shiva remembered.

I knew their Aunt Kobra. She lived in Ghom, a small city between Esfahan and Tehran. Since Ghom wasn't big, it didn't have an airport; flying to GHOM and then to Tehran wasn't an option anymore. Shiva had to think of an alternate plan, which would make it possible to stop in Ghom on her way to Tehran.

"I should travel by bus. I will reserve bus tickets to Ghom and from there to Tehran," Shiva said.

"Why would you want to go by bus? I will take you," Pooya offered.

"Well, thanks Pooya, but you really don't have to go through all that trouble."

"Look at it this way, see, if I drive you to Tehran, not only will I be with you all the way, but I can visit Aunt Kobra, too. Don't you agree, Fariba? We can all go together."

"Darling, your car is small and all of us can't travel in your car. But it is a good idea if you can take Shiva and your nephews," I replied.

"I can rent a bigger car."

"No, Pooya, it's not necessary. Sepideh and I will stay here. You go and have fun."

"I don't know…I don't want to leave you two here."

"We'll be fine, right, Sepideh?"

"Right, I'll take care of mommy until you come back."

"I feel awful now. I don't want to cause any problems. Maybe it is better if I just fly to Tehran and forget about Aunt Kobra?" Shiva said.

"Don't be silly. Pooya can take some time off from my nagging," I said jokingly.

"I will take your nagging anytime, darling," Pooya answered as he kissed me.

"Well, no more of this talk. It's settled. You, your sister and your nephews go and have a wonderful traveling time. That's an order."

"Yes, my dear," Pooya said laughing.

~

few days later, they left Esfahan for Ghom.

"I'll be back soon, darling," Pooya promised.

"Don't worry about Sepideh and me. We'll be fine. Take care of yourself," I told him as I hugged him real hard and kissed him tenderly.

Pooya and I had never been apart since my first trip home to see Papa. I knew it would be hard not having him around for a couple of days, but, 'we can manage,' I thought. Plus, I wanted Pooya to spend as much time as he could with Shiva and bringing her to Tehran seemed to be a good plan.

When they left, I watched his car as Sepideh waved goodbye. I watched them until his car disappeared into the curve on the next street. I looked at the sky and saw a big dark cloud over our house.

"Let's go inside, Sepideh. It looks like it's going to rain soon," I told her.

That day, my dear, what can I tell you? That day, I kissed my Pooya for the last time and never saw him again. He never came back to me. He died in a car crash on his way back home to us. I lost him for the second time. He died twice in one lifetime. No chance of returning, no hope, because it really happened. No 'falsely assumed,' he really died and I knew with that, a love story had come to an end. I knew that I'd lost Pooya for good, no mistaken identity this time; you know why? Because I identified his body myself.

I didn't believe it at first. I didn't want to believe.

"It's happened before," I told them. "They had told me that he was dead in the past, but he wasn't," I explained. "I want to see him for myself."

Another chapter had closed itself from my life. The chapter I wanted to leave open until the end. I didn't want to be Pooya's survivor. I didn't want this to be over. I still wanted to write more and forever on that chapter. I still had things to say to Pooya, things to do with him. I wanted that page to stay open for eternity. Gone too soon was an unfinished story of a love bigger than life itself. The story of an angel who saved me, loved me. Not a mortal love, but an immortal, heavenly love.

After that, I had to stay strong for Sepideh one more time. I had to fight the desire to die. I had to stay alive to make sure Sepideh lived the life she deserved and so I did stay alive. One more time, I survived his loss.

Sometimes I think of the strength God gives people so they can just go on. I was like a tree, which had bent so many times with so many storms, but never broke; I stood right up straight to stare the storm in the eye. But I also know that Pooya's hand on my back had always given me the support I needed. Maybe I had been a tree, but he had been the root within me. In reality, he had never left me.

"Pooya is still alive; he lives in me, in my heart and in my dreams, just like before. He lives in this house, I can smell him and then I know he's here. That's one of the reasons I never left this house. He comes to visit. He has his ways to show me that he was here. Only I can see the signs and can smell his scent. Yes, my dear, he lives here with me."

~

As I left Grandma Fariba, I couldn't help not thinking about her story. Her story had touched me beyond belief. Pooya, the man whom I never had an opportunity to meet, had been at the core of her life. Perhaps he was an angel, or maybe just a man whose heart held all the love in the world for one woman. Perhaps he was a savior, or maybe just an ordinary man…who died twice.

The end